ANN HIATT

BET ON yourself

Recognize, Own, and Implement Breakthrough Opportunities

HarperCollins
LEADERSHIP

AN IMPRINT OF HarperCollins

For entrepreneurs everywhere

Published by HarperCollins Leadership, an imprint of
HarperCollins Focus LLC.

Any internet addresses, phone numbers, or company or product information
printed in this book are offered as a resource and are not intended in any
way to be or to imply an endorsement by HarperCollins Leadership,
nor does HarperCollins Leadership vouch for the existence, content,
or services of these sites, phone numbers, companies, or products
beyond the life of this book.

ISBN 978-1-4002-2030-4 (eBook)
ISBN 978-1-4002-2026-7 (HC)

Library of Congress Control Number: 2021941747

Printed in the United States of America
21 22 23 24 5 LSC 10 9 8 7 6 5 4 3 2 1

TABLE OF CONTENTS

FOREWORD

*E*veryone can remember a similar feeling when the COVID-19 pandemic took hold: a sense that many things were no longer under control. As the virus spread around the globe, parts of daily life that many had taken for granted before were gone. Working in an office, gathering with loved ones, attending events, and traveling were out the window as staying healthy became the foremost concern. As I write this in June 2021, that feeling is ending thanks to advances in science and technology and the invention of life-saving vaccines. People are getting more control over their lives—and what comes next can be a once-in-a-century chance for reinvention.

How can we seize these kinds of moments? A variation of that question has probably dawned on all of us. We need advice. My former chief of staff and dear friend Ann Hiatt reminds us in these pages that "pivots are part of every life and career; whether intentional or not." Change is constant. The pivot to a post-pandemic world will be historic, but it won't be the last shift in our lives.

Turning these pivots into opportunities requires a strategy to reimagine what's possible. That strategy could include reflecting on fundamentals, rethinking priorities, and asking ourselves what we value and why. This is not an easy task. A book with great stories about a life full of changes, challenges, and purpose—a book that shows tanglible ways we can all find meaning—couldn't be timelier. And it starts by giving the advice that so many need to hear after so much has been out of our control—*Bet on Yourself*.

Ann was on her way to becoming a Scandinavian studies professor, not the chief of staff at Google, a speaker, and a leadership strategist, when a persistent recruiter gave her a call in 2006. The recruiter had to pick up the phone three more times before Ann even agreed to tour Google's campus, let alone leave her PhD program. But that persistence paid off, and Ann took a bet on herself that she was the person our team needed to accomplish our mission through some of the most important years of my career and Google's history. That bet made all the difference.

Before Ann and I worked together, she had established a reputation built on excellence without ego. She always did her homework. She had a track record of being a force multiplier for those around her—an ability she may have picked up as the oldest of seven children descended from Idaho farmers and an Air Force pilot based in Alaska, who flew F-4 Phantom fighter jets. She could be in several places at once, managing projects in London and New York while spearheading the team at our headquarters in California. Most importantly, she empowered and elevated her teammates to pursue excellence.

How she did all this has often been a mystery. But in reading this book, her method and dedication come through. Each chapter goes through case studies and business lessons from her career and then invites the reader to apply them in their own lives through an ROI sprint, wherein you Recognize, Own, and Implement your own course toward a rewarding professional and personal life. These ROI sprints demonstrate that the lessons we learned in Silicon Valley are applicable in any field.

That's especially true for those of us who want to use opportunities for reinvention to achieve new goals. Three years into our partnership, Ann entered my office with the objective of taking the next big step in her career. She was ready to be chief of staff. She had a habit of laying out clear objectives six months or a year in advance, but this was different. The role of "chief of staff" didn't yet exist. So, she invented it. She put together a roadmap of what the role could look like and how she could develop the skills to take our operation to the next level. What I didn't fully appreciate before *Bet on Yourself* was the legwork Ann did to find new ways to make meaningful contributions—it involved a lot of spreadsheets. The template she outlines can help you take a proactive approach to your career and chart your growth, no matter what business you're in. Today, the role of "chief of staff" is standard in the technology industry.

This book also contains stories of some of the mistakes we made along the way—some serious and some we now laugh about. An anecdote in the latter category came to mind when I read Ann's discussion of her rituals to build resilience, including her commitment to work out every morning. She was gracious enough not to include this, but when I made a commitment to become fitter during my tenure, I went with her to one of her dawn high-intensity interval training classes. It was in the company parking lot, where our colleagues pulled into work. That day, they got to see me embody Google's emphasis on "failing early and often," as I struggled to keep up while the sun rose. I may not have gone back to the class the next day, but Ann's right that challenging ourselves builds resilience. We all need new challenges.

Resilience was necessary in 2011, when I became the executive chairman of Google after 10 years as CEO. I wanted to take the opportunity to reimagine what leadership could look like. Every one of my direct reports assumed new roles, except for one. Ann became the only person who reported directly to me as we entered this new phase. With just a small team after the reorganization, Ann created what I later described as an "embarrassingly good" operation. In this book, she goes through chapter and verse how she made that happen—from the structure to the staffing to the ethos of collaboration and information-sharing.

Making sure that we all understood we were on a team and had one another's backs was very important. In 2017, I gave a speech where I was followed by the newly elected president of France, Emmanuel Macron. Ann noticed I was on edge, which wasn't typical. But the truth is, I was on edge. Not only was it a high-profile event, but the world was going through significant changes that made us all uncertain about the future. I wanted to convey some counterintuitive hope about topics that worry many people, especially the rapid pace of technological progress. Ann's steady presence and the sense that we were on a team helped me to deliver that message at a time when it needed to be heard.

Bill Campbell, the coach to some of the most powerful executives in Silicon Valley, taught me, "Your title makes you a manager, but it's your team that makes you a leader." As we pivot toward a post-pandemic future with a chance for reinvention, the world needs good leaders. From someone who's dedicated her career to bringing out greatness in those around her and in herself, I can't think of a more fitting contribution to that cause than *Bet on Yourself*.

—Eric Schmidt, cofounder, Schmidt Futures,
and former CEO and executive chairman, Google

INTRODUCTION

*I*n 2003, I almost killed Jeff Bezos. Thankfully, that wasn't the end of that story or of my career.

In this book, I will share with you this and other stories that you will not hear anywhere else. My career has woven a rare path through a unique period of time and a cast of characters that can never be replicated. I have spent decades at the side of not one but three highly influential CEOs, who built the foundation of Amazon and Google. While you might have picked up this book for the stories behind these exceptionally impactful companies and people, and the unique Silicon Valley environment, I hope that what keeps you coming back to this book are the lessons and inspiration that will awaken something in your own life and career.

This book is also an attempt to answer the question of why each of these three CEOs—Jeff Bezos, Marissa Mayer, and Eric Schmidt—chose me to be their right-hand partner in executing their vision across periods of high stakes and rapid growth. I'll share some ways I've discovered to make my work and collaboration style set these high impact CEOs up to do their best work. You'll also hear how I've discovered a way to have a catalyst-like effect in our partnerships that contributed to them achieving their legendary successes. I now want to do the same for *you*!

The heart and soul of this book has the individual contributor in mind. I want you to walk away from this time we share together feeling more in control of your destiny and better able to reinvest in and reinvent yourself. Opportunities are all around you when you know what to look for!

If you are currently in a leadership position, this book will not only illustrate the incredible patterns of leadership and best practices I've absorbed from each of my CEO bosses but will illustrate the types of employees you will want to attract, motivate, and invest in for your team. You will be inspired to find your own force multipliers to bring out the best in your work. I spent twelve years at Google—which in tech years is more like one hundred years! I did so because I was able to reinvent myself over and over within that environment, rather than having to look outside the company for advancement or learning opportunities. This book will show you the types of environments to create that empower this type of employee to continually level up and bring exceptional results.

Mine is a story of trial and error. This book is an accounting of my journey of not only watching history being made at the beginning of the internet but being brave enough to create my own role in it. I do want to acknowledge that luck and privilege were a huge part in the foundation of my journey. I was blessed to be born to a family that could afford to encourage and invest in my education. I grew up in a nice neighborhood, where innovation was happening outside my front door. Even my traditionally Scandinavian appearance made my hard work statistically more likely to be rewarded. I didn't earn that. But I hope that some of the hard work, experimentation, and pivoting I did feel applicable and inspire parts of your journey, no matter where you're coming from.

We will come back to the details of that fateful day in 2003 when I almost killed Jeff Bezos in a later chapter, but let me tell you now that in that trial by fire I learned that I could either shrink from challenges and failure or choose to become resilient and lead. I have experienced adventures, challenges, heartaches, embarrassments, and victories more extreme than I ever could have imagined.

You don't need to live in Silicon Valley or report directly to billionaire CEOs or attend an Ivy League school in order to open the doors to your dreams or benefit from their methods. This book is for anyone who has big dreams or who simply has a gut feeling that he or she is made for more.

Do you long for something different or bigger for your life? You might be starting your first job and wondering how you can use it as a stepping stone toward your dream career. Or you might be midcareer and want to finally be recognized for promotion or a leadership role. Perhaps your main goal is to feel more empowered, respected, and valued for your contributions. Do you have an audacious dream that no one around you fully understands? I am here to help you do it!

I will show you how to recognize and explore opportunities for advancement when options might appear limited at first. I will show you how to adopt the mindset of fearless change-makers and empower you to own your big dreams and work toward them unapologetically.

In this book, I will use my own career as a case study. Not because I am perfect by any stretch; I do so because when we look at seemingly wildly successful people, they can feel unrelatable and their results so unattainable that we opt out of even attempting to replicate their paths. I am sharing my story to illustrate how I have translated the best practices of some of the most successful people in business for the rest of us "normal people." The leadership principles that guide their work are, in fact, directly applicable to your goals and career.

This book presents a unique perspective that not even my CEO bosses could give you. I have synthesized the common threads that weave their best practices all together into a single playbook. No one else has witnessed all three of these highly successful tech pioneers navigate these irreplicable challenges and moments in time as I have.

This book is not hero worship. The companies and leaders I have worked for are not perfect, and I wouldn't want to pretend that they are. However, there are some universal truths that I've extracted from each experience to give a template for creating big results. This book also won't include any juicy behind-the-scenes gossip—I don't have any!

I wrote this book because I believe strongly in democratizing the internet and bringing as many underrepresented voices to the forefront as possible. I also believe in the democratization of success. The secrets of Silicon Valley success shouldn't only be for the elite. These best practices can help anyone, at any growth stage, reach his or her potential and achieve greatness.

More than ever, the world needs you. We need you to commit to building the future that you are uniquely capable of creating. We need more voices, more perspectives, more insights, and more diversity of experiences to create a future that is full of hope, joy, and peace for our shared world. The sooner you own your place in that process, the sooner we all benefit.

With a few consistent, daily habits, you can create your dream life. You can build a legacy you are proud of. Even though the opportunities available to you in your particular community or career stage may seem limited, there is a path you can forge to create a life you love. In the pages that follow, you will find tools you can use to give you control of your life and destiny.

In this book, you will:

- Learn to focus your mindset, prioritizing learning over perfect performance and finding more meaning and satisfaction in your work.
- Identify ways to have more impact, even if you currently have little to no formal power.
- Build a network of peers and mentors to support and inspire you as you take calculated risks.
- Discover your personal leadership strengths and seek out ways to grow and take on projects that relate more closely to your values, so that your life is passion-based and fulfilling.
- Learn to build a firm foundation from your expertise, confidence, and experiences, from which you can draw strength and clear direction.
- Discover how to once and for all stop being overlooked for promotion, investment, leadership opportunities, and passion projects.
- Learn to manage up and teach your leadership teams and peers to see you and your potential clearly—even if you're still developing as you go.

This book will walk you through the process of Recognizing, Owning, and Implementing these concepts, which will give you the formula for your personal ROI to be recognized for your ambition, be seen as a leader, and collect the right sponsors and mentors.

At the end of each chapter, you will find an ROI Sprint. These are challenges that will help you apply the business lessons discussed in the chapter to your own life today. Sprints are a pervasive practice in tech companies. They are a repeated series of timeboxed, focused work for developing, delivering, and sustaining complex goals. Marathon-length goals can feel intimidating, and it can seem impossible to know how to get started. Sprints are how we consistently build, step by step, toward our larger goals. This is how you reverse engineer your moonshot dreams and demand more satisfaction in your work.

I will show you how to create a roadmap to your dream career and a proud, empowered, and joyful future self. You will be the hero of your own life and an inspiration to everyone around you.

Are you ready? It's time to bet on yourself! Let's get started!

BET ON yourself

FOUNDATION BUILDING

I am a first-generation nonfarmer in my family. The fact that I have built a career in the most influential technology companies in the world, working side by side with the wealthiest and most powerful CEOs, is nothing short of shocking. I have always wanted to have a life and career of significance, but that dream has taken shape in unexpected ways.

The secret to happiness is learning to find joy in the process of doing hard things. I am lucky to have had this principle first modeled for me in my early childhood. My family history is full of stories of people who took very limited resources and, with a lot of hard work and creative allocation, created lives of joy and meaning. No one in my family has been significantly powerful or wealthy, but they consistently have exhibited a pattern of creating results that are greater than the sum of the parts.

I was taught early in life that there is exponential power in the combination of hard work and big dreams. When I look back at my upbringing, I see the ways in which I was prepared to survive and then thrive in my unexpected career.

These foundational principles can be applied to any life, goal, or growth stage to yield big results:

- Recognize the exponential power of hard work and big dreams.
- Create environments for growth.
- Embrace incremental growth.

No life is too small and no dream too big to be worthy of investment. Even if you're at the beginning of your career and your current job in no way represents your dream job, this is the perfect moment to create a map for yourself so that you can recognize opportunities and seize moments for advancement that might pass you by if you aren't watching and preparing for them. This is how you engineer serendipity!

In order to understand how my life could become successfully intertwined with the CEOs of Amazon and Google, it's important to understand a bit about me and my background.

RECOGNIZE THE EXPONENTIAL POWER OF HARD WORK AND BIG DREAMS

I come from a long line of dreamers.

My early life shaped my future, of course, but I am only now coming to realize the ways and degrees to which that's true. I am the firstborn in my family of seven children. My parents both grew up on potato farms in Idaho, where they also herded sheep.

My great-grandparents emigrated from Scandinavia and Switzerland, dreaming of better opportunities in America and fully believing in their abilities to create a life of limitless possibilities in the New World.

Similarly, my dad, Glade, is also a man of big dreams. He saw the toll that the hard farming life took on his father and decided that the stress and heart attacks that awaited him in that life were not what he wanted. He and his three brothers are all incredibly smart. My dad studied accounting as an undergraduate, figuring that was a sure way of providing for a family in the future, but his heart wasn't in it. He wanted to fly, but not just in any plane: he wanted to be a fighter pilot.

The chances of not washing out of pilot training and then being chosen as a member of the elite graduates who got to be fighter pilots were astronomically small, but my dad was determined and confident that he would beat the odds. His journey was an example of boldness, purpose, and bravery. He had to let go of everything familiar and make a big bet on himself—and it paid off.

I was born on MacDill Air Force Base in Tampa, Florida, just after my father had finished pilot training and was chosen to fly the F-4 Phantom fighter jet. Being born into a military family forged something in me. My siblings and I grew up feeling we had no choice but to adapt to circumstance and to be self-reliant and brave in the face of unpredictable schedules, assignments, and events.

Goose's Daughter

When I was a year old, my family was transferred from Florida to Anchorage, Alaska. It was the tail end of the détente period of the

Cold War, and my father's squadron was tasked with patrolling and protecting the airspace between Alaska and the easternmost part of the Soviet Union. Among my earliest memories is one of looking up into the sky from our backyard with my sister LaDawn watching the fighter planes overhead, and trying to guess which one was Dad.

While we were stationed in Alaska, a movie studio had commissioned a script about fighter pilots, and they asked the US Air Force if they could listen to cockpit recordings so that they could better re-create the way fighter pilots talk to each other. The Air Force gave permission and provided them with transcripts from my father's flight squadron, the Hornets.

A few years later, when the movie was ready to be released, the Air Force had second thoughts: they grew nervous about the way pilots were portrayed, so they withdrew their permission previously granted to the movie producers to refer to their characters as Air Force pilots. The Navy, it turns out, didn't have the same reservations, so the script was slightly changed. While the Air Force references were removed, they kept the original lingo and the call sign names of the pilots that were heard in the cockpit recordings.

That movie was *Top Gun*. My father's military call sign was Goose, and I spent my childhood with Maverick, Ice Man, and others who are now minor legends because of that movie. I didn't see *Top Gun* until I was in college because my dad didn't like that they made his namesake a navigator rather than a pilot, or that they killed off his character. He *did* like that they emphasized that he was a good family man, which he is.

Something happens to you when you are Goose's daughter. You learn to go after bold dreams even when everyone around you (you, too, sometimes) thinks they're crazy. I learned to be purposeful and to work hard every day for a goal that might not be attainable but that was worth the risk to try. Most of all, I learned to be brave. My dad lost close colleagues in his squadron, men killed in training accidents while we were living in officers' quarters on base. My mom told us of the terror she felt watching officers in full dress uniforms arrive in our neighborhood, and of all the wives opening their doors in growing horror, hoping that it wasn't their turn, that the officers would not stop in front of their houses.

The experience instilled in me a drive to appreciate fully the value of every day and to be intentional in how I chose to spend my time. No day is to be wasted—not one. Every good morning kiss and hug—each and every one—is to be savored.

Creative Resilience

While my dad was fulfilling his childhood dreams flying multimillion-dollar jets and becoming a movie legend, my mom, Tammy, was at home, thousands of miles from her parents, siblings, family, friends, and comfort zone she'd grown up with in Idaho. But my mother has never been one to shy away from a challenge. She took after her parents, who were tireless farmers, active community members, and talented artists who enjoyed painting landscapes in their free time.

She planted these lessons learned on her Idaho family farm—of hard work, creativity, and community—deep into my childhood home in Alaska. She created a preschool program for our neighborhood to help us make friends and build a support system. She took ceramics classes and painted oil paintings inspired by the magnificent wilderness around us. She took us fishing and berry picking in the mountains with bells tied to our little shoes so we wouldn't surprise any bears.

In those early years, I learned to take the initiative to create inspiring, enriching environments where others might see only limitations. My mom taught me to create extraordinary things from the ordinary.

There were unparalleled adventures as well as big challenges that came with my childhood. Both the nature and nurture sides of my early years cultivated important personality traits. Growing up as an Air Force brat shaped my personality and instincts. I learned to be resourceful in unknown environments, and with limited resources. Moving frequently taught me to be adaptable and (ideally) unflappable.

While shy by nature, I learned a love of adventure, exploring the unknown rather than being intimidated by it. In school I was never the one to raise my hand, though I very often knew the answer; over time I have learned to overcome my instinct to never say anything aloud until I had a fully formed, perfected idea. I'm definitely still a work in progress! Some of my natural qualities are my greatest strengths. Some I actively fight to this day.

My childhood is an example of learning to bet on yourself. My dad took a purposeful, calculated risk to leave his familiar farm life and submit himself to the judgment, failures, and challenges inherent in pilot training. My mother's challenges came from the life circumstances of a military spouse. They both successfully used these challenges to fulfil their dreams, where others around them had been too afraid to even make an attempt.

Sacrifice and growth are inseparably linked. We have to be brave enough to let go of something we have now in hopes of something greater taking its place in the future.

This principle is illustrated well in Robert Pirsig's philosophical novel *Zen and the Art of Motorcycle Maintenance*, where he describes the concept of the Monkey Trap. The trap is simply a hollowed-out coconut shell, filled with tempting rice, with a hole just big enough for a monkey's hand to slip through. A monkey reaches in and fills his hand with rice, but his clenched fist is too big to pull back out. The monkey is effectively trapped by his own choice because he will not let go of the rice in order to free himself from the shell, which is chained to the ground.

Human nature is very similar. Often we are unwilling to let go of our unfulfilling jobs, relationships, or responsibilities because they're familiar and seem less risky than letting them go in hopes that the sacrificed safety will be rewarded with something greater. Too often we find ourselves clutching a handful of symbolic rice and not realizing that we're trading in our freedom for something that we cannot even enjoy.

Years later, when my dad made the hard decision to leave the military with the goal of spending more time with our family, we were three daughters with a fourth on the way. Dad would need to make a living, of course, so he enrolled in law school, also working part-time as a janitor to make ends meet. That was quite a comedown from his previous standing as an elite fighter pilot, but he was willing to make that sacrifice for the benefit of the future of our family.

This was another impactful example of the humility and wisdom required to let go of the seeming grandeur of an accomplished dream in order to open yourself up to a new aspiration. Joy and opportunity diminish if you hang on to old laurels too long. Your kinetic energy is drained when you are stagnant.

CREATE ENVIRONMENTS FOR GROWTH

My ambitions have always exceeded my natural abilities, and it wasn't until recently that I discovered that this has been my greatest advantage all along. This imbalance forced me to fight for everything I really wanted, which made me accustomed to pursuing things that were difficult to achieve. I think if I had been born with any naturally great abilities, I would have rested on those gifts and not pushed myself to the extent necessary to go beyond them.

The comfort of the *good* can rob us of the drive for the *exceptional*.

My family's next move halfway across the country changed the course of my life. After completing a judicial clerkship, my dad accepted a job offer with a law firm in Seattle—but my parents didn't want to live in the "big city," so they bought a house in Redmond, Washington, on Education Hill, where our elementary, junior high, and high schools were all within a short walk from our home. We had a big yard and a garden, which were very important to my parents.

Unintentionally that decision meant that I grew up in the epicenter of the new digital era, surrounded by the pioneer entrepreneurs and moonshot thinkers in the local tech scene during the eighties and nineties. My parents didn't give a thought to the fact that the headquarters of what would become arguably the most successful companies in the world were just a short drive from our front door.

My role as the oldest sibling of seven has followed me into my adult life and even my career. I have always had to be very organized, a self-starter, and a peacekeeper. It was—and is—the only way to be heard in crowded, fast-paced environments.

My parents instilled in me their farm-raised work ethic and drive to aim for perfection and big dreams. From my dad I inherited my left-brained analytical skills and boldness in goal setting. From my mom I got my emotional intelligence, creative problem-solving, and compassion for others in times of struggle.

Overcoming Perfectionist Paralysis

I was a serious kid from the start and was self-critical from an early age. My standards for myself often exceeded those of my parents. I wanted top grades, to always be the lead in the school play, to be the perfect ballerina, and eventually to attend a top university, which would naturally lead me to a job with global impact.

At first the difference between my dreams and my natural abilities paralyzed me. It always felt like I had to work twice as hard as my peers just to keep up, and that made me self-conscious, doubtful, and willing to shrink into the background. Maybe that's how everyone feels during their teenage years, but it was crippling for me. I had an internal drive to make up for a lack of standout talent by outworking everyone, but at first I lacked the confidence that it would make a difference. My mom used to set an alarm for 1:00 a.m.—not to see if I had snuck out with friends, but to be sure I had put away my homework and actually went to bed.

I had absorbed the lesson—too deeply, at times, I admit—of being purposeful in everything I did. I have always felt a burning for something more, and I imagine this is even more true for those who begin with few advantages and resources. I was like my dad, who started out by milking cows before daybreak and dreaming of flying fighter jets before he had ever laid eyes on one in person.

This crippling anxiety of never doing anything truly special or important might have been my fate if it weren't for a very special teacher. My junior high choir conductor, Ron Mahan, was very influential in my life. He saw this fear in me and encouraged me to overcome it. He helped me move into a growth mindset, believing that my talents weren't fixed and that with effort I could improve over time. At the end of eighth grade, which had been a particularly traumatic year of social anxiety for me, when I asked him to sign my yearbook, he instead pulled out a prewritten card and placed it inside.

The note encouraged me to approach every challenge with confidence rather than preconceived failure. Until that moment, I hadn't realized that I was doing that—self-sabotaging—and in effect sealing my fate of a disappointing performance. He told me that I should hold my head high because I was already great. Most importantly, in the next school year, he followed that up with opportunities to prove to myself that I didn't have to be perfect in order to be proud of myself and shine. He gave me solo parts that I felt I didn't deserve, but I wanted to make him proud so I worked hard to improve. His belief that I could be special allowed me to believe it too.

This was an enormous mental shift for my young mind. I could create my own luck.

Determination Trumps Natural Talent

Learning to bet on myself in my younger years was an incremental, rather than exponential, process. It taught me how to recognize calculated risks and to be brave enough to take a running jump off the diving board even if I belly flopped a few times first.

I guess I hadn't realized until then that you can just climb back up the ladder and try again, armed with new knowledge about what not to do. A single failure to meet a goal isn't an eternal state of being unless you choose to make it so.

It is human nature to avoid embarrassment, pain, or discomfort, but often the anticipation of these moments is worse than the actual experience itself. Life's greatest joys come when we recognize which opportunities will bring us the greatest growth in return for stretching beyond the limits of our comfort zone. You can engineer radical growth for yourself when you realize the relationship between risk-taking and learning. If you can value learning as a center of your development and life satisfaction, you're able to offset the fear of trying something new.

The key for me in learning to be comfortable with being uncomfortable with a new challenge has been in learning to equate new things with excitement and reward rather than fear and failure. Like with any muscle, it takes time and heavy repetition to build up tolerance and strength. While I learned this lesson early in life, I have had to relearn it many times over.

EMBRACE INCREMENTAL GROWTH

My first "real" job was given to me under somewhat false pretenses. In 1995, one of my best friends in high school, Melissa, worked at a start-up—back when few people even knew what a start-up was—and recommended me for her job when her family was moving from Washington State to North Carolina. I was sixteen and had just gotten my driver's license. I had to choose that fall between being in the school play, *Noises Off*, or starting a part-time job after school.

As the oldest of seven kids, I needed to start saving money for college, so I chose to start working. I had decided that I absolutely did not want a job that involved food or a cash register, which significantly limited the options for a teenager. So when Melissa asked me if I wanted to take over as office manager at Musicware, a mere ten-minute drive from my house in Redmond, I was thrilled.

Musicware was founded by two brothers who had recently graduated from Harvard Business School. They had created a software program for music transcription where musicians could play their compositions into an electronic keyboard and the software would transcribe the sheet music automatically. The software also offered piano lessons that would automatically detect how you were performing and suggest exercises to improve your skills. It was pretty impressive for 1995.

Melissa and I had sung together in school choirs since the sixth grade, and we were both passionate about music. While she was an accomplished pianist, I knew only enough to play my part off of sheet music, with one finger. While her primary responsibilities at Musicware were typical office manager duties, she also did beta testing of the software. When she recommended me for the job, she failed to tell them about the discrepancies in our piano skills.

Building Confidence

It soon became obvious to me that I lacked most of the skills the job required. Musicware was just a five-person company, so there was no one to train or mentor me. Other than babysitting, I had never had a job before and had no clue what was expected of me.

But I knew I was a hard worker, and I trusted that I could figure it out, so I put my head down and got to work.

I focused on learning how to run an office and wearing the many hats required in that role, but what interested me most was watching the brother-founders run the company, how they were learning as they were doing. They subscribed to business magazines I hadn't known existed (such as *Harvard Business Review*, *Fortune*, and *Fast Company*, which had just launched in 1995), and I started reading them cover to cover during my breaks. Yes, I was a weird kid. Working for these start-up founders was my first exposure to the possibilities of the business world.

I listened intently to the founders' conversations about how to make the most of their investment. I was fascinated! I did my best to look like I was "testing" the software while actually using it to develop my own piano skills enough to be helpful with its more advanced features. I wish I could report that I was a savant and learned to play the piano expertly during my two years working there after school. However, I definitely improved, and I even logged a few bugs along the way.

I built up my confidence enough that the company eventually sent me to do sales demos at Costco on the weekends. That was terrifying! I was painfully shy back then, and the idea of approaching strangers and trying to make sales was not my idea of a good time. I remember the horror I felt when an eager potential customer approached me—the dream scenario for every salesperson!—and asked me to demonstrate how well the software had taught me to play. My performance was not very persuasive. I did not close the sale, but I did learn that rejection is not a death sentence.

During these early years at the start-up, I made more mistakes than I can remember and had to get used to constant constructive criticism. My natural inclination was to shy away from projects that I didn't know how to do and that put me at risk of failing.

But the wonderful thing about not having any idea how to do any part of my job well was that I could not run from it. I couldn't hide my weaknesses by putting all my attention into what I did well and just avoiding those things I struggled with. That "luxury" comes later in your career. (Though, as I would learn, that's when you need to fight that urge the most!)

I had to lean into the discomfort of not being perfect, and only then did I realize that it *didn't actually matter*. All my bosses saw was someone trying her best and learning fast. I made a conscious effort to stop being so afraid of not being perfect. I was liberated by letting go of the expectation that perfection was the goal.

That was a turning point.

Becoming Team-Minded

While at Musicware, I learned to think on my feet, and to understand the importance of tasks that I was given. I still cringe thinking back to one of my first projects there. The founders asked me to assemble information packets about the business to send to potential buyers and customers. All I had to do was print out copies of ten documents and collate them into packets ready to mail. I didn't pay attention when the printer was acting up one day and produced hundreds of blurry, unprofessional-quality copies. The founder came to me and told me to throw them all out and start again.

My only focus had been on getting this mindless task finished only so I could spend time on the tasks that I enjoyed more (like eavesdropping on business-strategy meetings). However, I hadn't thought about the purpose of the project or what it would say to the sales leads if they received my shoddy work. I wasn't representing the values of the company. I had wasted company resources in the process. That was a pivotal realization. I still feel embarrassed about that episode, but I have never repeated that mistake.

After that experience, when given a task, especially a deceptively simple one, I always stepped back and thought about the larger picture—the purpose and the end result or end user—and how I could deliver on the mission rather than just the task. This created a drive and focus to maximize even the smallest tasks. I have often reflected on the words of Martin Luther King Jr., when he said, "If it falls your lot to be a street sweeper, sweep streets like Michelangelo painted pictures. Sweep streets like Beethoven composed music. Sweep streets like Leontyne Price sings before the Metropolitan Opera. Sweep streets like Shakespeare wrote poetry. Sweep streets so well that all the hosts of heaven and earth will have to pause and say, 'Here lived a great street sweeper who swept his job well.'" That is how you create your own opportunities out of limited resources and get noticed! Had I not learned that lesson when young, I would have been unprepared for the life-changing opportunities to come.

It's a mistake to discount our lives, responsibilities, or goals as too small to be significant or worthy of investment. These measured efforts add up over time and build the kinetic energy we need to do something bigger than we had originally dared to dream. No one takes their first dive off of the ten-meter platform! However, don't assume your fate will forever be in the kiddie pool.

My work at Musicware taught me how important it was to understand how my work fit into the larger mission of the company and contributed to my coworkers' abilities to perform at their best and meet our shared goals of financial viability. I saw for the first time how important it was to synchronize our energy and efforts across the team. I realized that my assignments weren't going to come neatly wrapped up with a full explanation from my manager about what the larger problem was that I was actually being tasked to solve. It was my own responsibility to define what success really meant for seemingly small tasks within the scope of what the company was trying to accomplish.

If I had framed the assignment of creating the information packets for Musicware in a way where I understood that the successful outcome of this task was actually to convert interest into sales and making the company profitable, then I would have been more thoughtful in regards to the quality of the work I was producing and made sure it represented the company in the best way. With this framework in mind, the task that had originally seemed lowly and unimportant now was perhaps the most important thing happening in the company that day.

I am lucky to have learned so early in my career the need to empower myself by asking the right questions so I can understand the higher purpose for each of my tasks. This has been the key for me to be able to consistently produce the right results and offer innovative solutions, especially when I was inexperienced or contributing outside my area of expertise later in my career. The secret to how anyone can become indispensable to their team and company, regardless of their role or seniority, is to properly orient their work responsibilities within the context of the larger team goal. With this knowledge, anyone will consistently be able to work smarter and not just harder than others around them.

CHAPTER 1 ROI SPRINT

When pushing yourself out of your comfort zone to accomplish big goals and have enriching experiences, you have to take a pro-active approach. This requires active creativity and building up resilience through experimentation and some failure. Don't be afraid to start small and build incremental progress. These are the first steps to getting you closer to realizing your dreams.

Recognize: Have you been self-limiting your impact out of fear of failure or embarrassment? Is there a big dream you have yet to say out loud or give yourself permission to pursue? Is there someone on your team who could use your guidance and helping hand?

Own: In what ways can you take responsibility for your own luck today through hard work, asking strategic questions, and creatively using your talents and resources available to you?

Implement: Redefine your current role, responsibilities, projects, and tasks in ways that impact the bottom line of your company and center your work around critical growth areas.

CREATING CAREER OPPORTUNITIES

*P*eople always want to know how I got Jeff Bezos to take a chance and hire me to work directly for him at Amazon as my very first job out of college. I had no connections at the company, no computer science degree, and absolutely no experience working for a CEO. People also often want to know how I later got recruited from my PhD program at UC Berkeley by Google to work for Marissa Mayer as her executive business partner and then made my way up to being the chief of staff for Eric Schmidt, the company's CEO and then executive chairman. They're also curious how and why I then pivoted from Google to become the founder of my own global consulting company. The secret lies in how I got noticed, made a reputation that preceded me, and was successful in such demanding environments by building line upon line even from within easily invisible or underestimated roles early in my career. Those early stages of my career gave me the building blocks upon which I stand today.

My seemingly impossible career trajectory makes more sense when we step back from me as the case study and look at the values and methods tech companies use to evaluate candidates in general.

Both Amazon and Google consistently prioritize hiring for intelligence, grit, and passion rather than only a specific skill set. Their philosophy is that they can teach a smart person to do anything. What you cannot teach is ambition or grit.

While I will be the first to emphasize that I've experienced a lot of luck in my career evolution, there have been some key ways I have purposefully created breakthrough career opportunities. I've made sure to do the following:

- Seek out irreplicable opportunities
- Prioritize learning
- Find meaningful impact

My unexpected career path has taught me to value, over all else, seeking out and jumping deep into irreplicable opportunities when I'm lucky enough to find them. Once I do, I am willing to take huge risks because I know these efforts are the ones that might change my life.

For me this has consistently come in the form of being willing to be an early employee and embracing all the chaos that comes with that, in order to work directly for a leader I greatly admire and hope to emulate. I have also consistently prioritized roles that required me to learn an expertise or skill that was key to my career progression both in depth and very quickly. I cannot overemphasize how important it has been to prioritize what I could learn in a role more than what the job description said that I would be asked to do. I have consistently experienced how the core job tasks of any role are much more adaptable to the passions and talents of the individual employee than most people realize. Most importantly, I have looked for opportunities to have a meaningful impact in the world through my work. Passion alignment has carried me further and faster toward progression and happiness than isolated financial gain or fancy job titles ever could have.

Some of the most important moments I have chosen to bet on myself have been when pursuing a new role. There is much more natural energy available when I am starting something new than when I am sitting in a comfortable role that I have already mastered.

SEEK OUT IRREPLICABLE OPPORTUNITIES

I first entered the job market during a tumultuous time. I graduated from the University of Washington, or UW, in 2002, just two years after the dot-com bust had wiped out trillions of dollars of investments and thousands of companies overnight, destroying the economy. I was excited about starting "the rest of my life" and embarking on unknown adventures despite the fact that employment options were limited and none of my classmates had internships or job offers after graduation.

I had co-majored at UW in international studies and Scandinavian studies and worked at the on-campus European Union Center, where I helped organize conferences to educate students and the community about European politics and business. The euro had been created in 1999 but wasn't formally adopted by the founding countries until 2002, my senior year of college, so that was a major theme of my student work.

The day-to-day tasks of my job at the EU Center were not glamorous, and I shared an office no bigger than a large closet with five others, but it gave me a gateway into understanding the global economy beyond just an academic perspective. It awakened an internal longing to be a part of that larger world and somehow help drive it—even though we were in the midst of a global financial crisis. My colleagues were all committed academics who opened up my world to the way in which academics and global politics translate into policies that shape cultures and communities.

My first boss at the EU Center, Phil Shekleton, used to get so intense when discussing these issues that he would tightly twist sections of his hair between his fingers and end every day looking like a kind of mad scientist. This was my introduction into how to think globally about my individual contributions. I found that idea thrilling. My job title was so insignificant that I don't think I even had one, and the pay was so small that I had to supplement it by also working at the Suzzallo Library reshelving books while studying full-time.

My original career goal was to be a professor and have an expert understanding of the major economic and political issues the world was facing. I was lucky to have two professors, Christine Ingebritsen and Lotta Gavel Adams, who saw potential in me and mentored me despite a lackluster start to my academic career in my freshman year. I leaned into, welcomed, and sought out their mentorship and was finally able to adapt to the university level and started to thrive. At the end of my four years at UW, I was awarded Best Senior Thesis from the Jackson School of International Studies. This turnaround gave me the confidence to believe that I might be able to accomplish my dream of a career in academics. Still, I felt like I needed a few years of "real world" work experience before I started my PhD studies.

That decision changed everything.

Willingness to Pivot

I asked the new director of the European Union Center what he thought I should do after graduation. "Have you thought about applying at Amazon?" he asked. His wife worked in recruiting there. No, I had not considered that. Growing up in Redmond, most of my friends' parents were tech executives, and, while they made good money, their lives didn't look particularly fun to me. However, the Seattle economy had been hit particularly hard by the dot-com bust, and most of my classmates were graduating without job offers, so I felt as if I should explore all options. I submitted my résumé to Amazon without much thought. To my surprise, I was called in for a first-round interview for a junior assistant role.

Looking back on that moment, what amazes me most is that I was able to see the possibility within that seemingly low-level job opportunity that was far detached from my career ambitions in academics. What many people misunderstand at the beginning of their career is that jobs that are the most fulfilling and rewarding rarely look like a dream job in the description.

What I was lucky enough to realize was that this seemingly unglamorous job title had the potential to expose me to things I never would have otherwise seen as a junior employee. This role could give me a purview into the backbone of how the company really ran and what was essential to its growth and success.

When I thought of this potential job opportunity through that lens, the role of a junior admin fit into my long-term growth plan perfectly. I had no idea how to be an assistant, but I knew that there was value in being consistently outside of my comfort zone and that I would be forced into an astronomical learning and growth curve, which would prepare me for the future roles I dreamed of having.

My initial interviews at Amazon were dizzying in volume and pace. I interviewed back-to-back with all of the senior assistants in the company. I was there all day and even had an interview over lunch, which meant that I didn't eat a thing. It became obvious to me that I hadn't prepared for these interviews in the right way. I had thought through my answers to the expected, typical interview questions, but I hadn't done any independent research on the company or their particular challenges. I hadn't prepared a list of questions to ask in return. In fact, I just got lucky that I had paid attention while waiting in the lobby and noted a display listing the five countries Amazon was then operating in. Less than five minutes later, an interviewer asked me if I used Amazon and if I knew where they were operating and expanding. My confident reply didn't let on that I had just learned the answer and had created my Amazon account the day before and hadn't yet made my first purchase. I went home exhausted but energized by the amazing people I met and from hearing about the pioneering projects they were working on. I felt immediately home in that environment.

Three months went by without a follow-up from Amazon.

I was exploring other opportunities that might be good preparation for my future PhD work when, to my surprise, I got a call to come in for a second round of interviews. This time I came deeply prepared after having read every single article I could about Amazon so that I could talk and ask questions confidently about the company's growth, challenges, and advantages in the evolving market. This time my interviews were with senior vice presidents of the company. I remember being confused about why they would spend executive time interviewing me, a very junior candidate.

One interview took place in a dark office with just the glow of a code-filled monitor and a weird multicolored rotating night-light in the corner. Unbeknownst to me, that executive had been assigned to find my breaking point and see if he could make me cry. Luckily I had known enough tech people in my life, so I was used to socially awkward interactions. I just chalked up the encounter to one of those personalities uniquely suited for the tech world and was unphased by it.

When three *more* months went by without a word, I was sure there was no way I was going to get a job at Amazon—and then the phone rang and the Amazon recruiter asked me to come back for one final interview. By this time I had been offered a job as a research assistant elsewhere, but I wasn't excited about it. I pointed out to the Amazon recruiter that she already possessed about twenty key data points on me and should therefore know if Amazon liked me or not without another round of exhausting interviews. I didn't want them kicking the decision down the road any longer. The recruiter apologized for the long, drawn-out process and promised me that this would be the final interview.

She did not tell me that it would be with Jeff Bezos himself.

I was willing to do a final round of interviews because Amazon had proven itself to be a company full of ambitious, dedicated, and passionate people. I wanted to be like them and learn what they knew. Their strengths were in the areas I personally wanted to develop, so the value of the experience was obvious even though it could have felt like a diversion from my academic goals.

I could feel that something was different about Amazon and that they were doing really hard things that no other company was attempting. I was sure that working there would teach me things I couldn't learn anywhere else. My entire goal in working before grad school was to get solid business experience, and this seemed like the perfect way to do so. So I returned a third time.

Trust Your Instincts

I felt relaxed going into the interview that October morning. Then suddenly the conference room door opened and Jeff entered, sat down, and let out his famously booming laugh before he even introduced himself. I recognized him immediately since his face was already in the local media almost daily.

At first I was confused. I thought that they had put me in the wrong room and that he was meant to interview an engineer or executive. But no, I was exactly where I was meant to be.

Jeff started the interview by promising that he was going to ask me only two questions—and the first one was a "fun" brainteaser. I took a deep breath as he stood and uncapped a pen at the whiteboard wall, in what turned out to be his personal conference room, and promised that he would do the math. I was momentarily terrified. "I want you to estimate the number of panes of glass in the city of Seattle," said Jeff.

No one had ever asked me a question like that before. I paused to calm down, reminding myself to think about his motivation for asking that question. *He wants to see the way my mind works,* I told myself. He wanted to see me break down a complicated problem into small, manageable steps.

I can do that, I thought.

I outlined how I would start with the number of people in the city of Seattle, which I thankfully correctly guessed as one million, just to make the math easier. Then I said that they would each have a home, a mode of transportation, and an office or school, all of which would have windows, so I suggested that we base the estimate on averages of those. And then we did the math.

We got down into every possible scenario, group, anomaly, and ways to account for these exceptions. It felt like I talked it through for hours while Jeff filled the whiteboard with numbers . . . I'm sure it actually took more like ten minutes. I remember feeling a thrill when he wrote down the final estimate. He circled it. "That looks about right," he said.

Phew!

Jeff then asked me the second question: he wanted to hear my career goals. Knowing Jeff as well as I do now, I see why these were his only two questions. He was measuring my potential by asking questions that would explore if I had the grit, courage, and motivation to run at his pace and be brave enough to consistently jump with him and level up. By the end of the interview, we both knew I would do anything to be successful despite being a very junior candidate.

And then I was done. Exhausted, exhilarated, done.

Jeff Bezos hired me on the spot. He gave me the open desk just three feet from his own. The closest desk in the company.

It took years for me to fully understand why Jeff took a chance on me and gave me this big break. Jeff exclusively surrounded himself with people he had to hold back, not push forward. He created teams of people so ambitious, creative, and determined that they made up for any expertise they lacked. In this environment, Jeff would only have to use his energy as a leader to channel our energy, rather than trying to pull it out of us. I learned that the key to Jeff's and Amazon's early success was this tireless pursuit of the exceptional.

Follow the Dreamers

Motivational speaker Jim Rohn famously said that we are the average of the five people we spend the most time with. I believe this to be true. This means that our work life will inevitably shape our personal life as well, since we spend the majority of our waking hours there. Our jobs can inspire us to aim higher, take on new challenges, and find increased satisfaction, or they can drain us, tear us down, and sap us of our joy and energy. It all comes down to the people surrounding us.

In every career move I've made since Amazon, I have made all of my job decisions based on the quality of people I would be working for and who they could teach me to become. That single piece of early wisdom has made all the difference in the happiness and evolution of my life.

The greatest gift of my life has been sitting next to the smartest CEOs in the world and learning step-by-step how they think, act, motivate, and make decisions. This was my first experience with an Olympic-level bet placed on myself. It would either make me or break me. I was willing to find out.

Ever since this early hiring experience, I have always aimed to be the person that needs to be held back, not pushed forward. I have sought out teams that would challenge, support, and inspire me to do things far beyond my current abilities, and that has led to more satisfaction in my work life than anything else. This has also made crushing workloads, terror around my subpar skill sets for an assigned task, and the constant need for up-leveling feel not only manageable but thrilling.

Place a Serious Bet

One of the most common denominators of the truly revolution-ary people I have encountered is that they are consistently willing to bet on themselves. They are willing to let go of a childhood dream if they find that an unexpected fork in the road better leads them to what they want to learn and contribute to the world. It is not that they are easily swayed; quite the contrary.

Extraordinary people are willing to let go of the expectations placed on them by family, society, and even their own childhood urgings in order to experience something truly fulfilling. They are willing to pivot even when their self-identity is on the line. This is true bravery and the largest predictor of long-term work/life satisfaction and impact.

Jeff had done this when he had the courage to quit his lucra-tive job at the New York–based hedge fund D.E. Shaw, where he worked for four years as the company's fourth senior vice presi-dent at the age of thirty. Jeff had many reasons to stay in that lane and continue to be rewarded handsomely for his hard work and big returns. He had no external reason to ditch all that and take a huge risk to start his own company.

In 1993, however, Jeff went to his boss and pitched his idea for an internet-based bookstore. He saw the exponential possibilities through this new technology. He could envision a store that was not limited by brick-and-mortar parameters and could house millions of products virtually. Jeff's headspace was in the future, and that is where breakthrough change occurs. For those whose headspace is in the present, they are solving current problems and their impact will be small. Jeff was solving for the needs of the future customer.

D. E. Shaw famously declined to invest in Jeff's idea. So he made a big bet on himself and quit his finance job to take a chance on this crazy new thing called the internet. Obviously, that worked out well for him in the end, but it required him to take a huge risk and bet his future on his ability to figure out things he had never done before. No one had!

I never expected that I would weave my own way through this process several times over the next decade. The first step in this unexpected journey was leaving Amazon to start my PhD after three years at the company. I adored my job at Amazon and cherished my time working with Jeff, but being in academia was my dream. It was agonizing for one dream to have to come to an end in order for another to begin.

Even now people ask me if it was the right decision to leave Amazon just when the company was becoming profitable and stock values were finally going up. But Jeff's enthusiastic reaction to the news of my acceptance into my PhD program at the University of California, Berkeley, reassured me that there is nothing better than investing in yourself. There is nothing more life changing than taking the chance to build your own dream rather than get paid to build someone else's—exactly as Jeff had done.

On my last day at Amazon, I brought my camera to work. I almost failed to summon the courage to ask Jeff if we could take a photo of the two of us together before I handed in my employee badge. I'm so thankful I did because that picture is one of my prized possessions today. I cried as I left the building.

I cried as I drove away from Seattle in my red Honda Civic full of boxes. I listened to the fourth Harry Potter book on CD for the two-day drive south to Berkeley, and I didn't absorb a word of it. Yet despite that enormous heartache and fear of the unknown, I remained sure that I wanted to follow Jeff's example and minimize my risk of future regret in not having taken a chance on myself and my dreams.

PRIORITIZE LEARNING

Beginning a PhD program is a humbling process. I was the only candidate admitted to the Scandinavian Studies program that year, so I had no one who was exactly a peer, going through what I was going through, at the same time and in the same program. My fellow PhD candidates were senior to me, so I felt as if I was the only person with no idea what was going on. This is where one of my most crucial Amazon experiences came in handy: learning to be comfortable as the most junior person in the room.

I clearly remember my first day arriving in the bare, sterile classroom on the second floor of Dwinelle Hall, in the center of Berkeley's campus, with only a single table in the center and five metal chairs around it. I was the only person who brought a laptop. My professor and two fellow graduate students just had backpacks full of books and paper notebooks. My professor did not lecture. She just led a discussion while seated next to me at the table.

I was also caught off guard by the kind of coursework that was expected of me. It resembled nothing like I had experienced as an undergraduate student. My dad had a master's degree and a law degree, so I simply expected my graduate school experience to model his, with a clear progression of exams to master. What I encountered instead were courses designed around consuming massive amounts of information, followed by three-hour-long sessions to discuss, debate, and pursue insights and perspectives based on the reading without any corresponding grades.

It felt very much as if I were joining a conversation that had begun a thousand years before I arrived and that would continue for another thousand after I departed. It was hard to know how to feel valuable and to measure if I was being successful because there weren't regular exams to use as benchmarks along the way.

At the end of my first semester, I stacked up all the books I had read, in four different languages: the pile towered over me. But I had no idea how to evaluate my actual performance in this environment. How could I know if I was doing well? Not understanding how to score my contribution or progression made me feel like the dumbest person in the room every day.

Learning for Learning's Sake

In truth, for that very reason, I was a terrible academic my first semester at Berkeley. My approach was far too rigidly analytical to benefit from just allowing concepts to wash over me and to have space to subconsciously inspire new perspectives. I wanted to run at an Amazon-inspired pace, which was mismatched with my department's goals of teaching me the value of learning for the value of opening the mind to new processes and perspectives without being tainted by other motivations. My personality type always wants to know what I'm going to learn or experience before it's even begun, and that is the opposite of the PhD experience! This disconnect was disorienting, and I struggled to apply everything I felt I had learned about how to be successful at Amazon into academics, which was slower and more nebulous.

I also felt mismatched in other ways. Although the Scandinavian Studies program at Berkeley was meant to be abroad, all of the current graduate students had a literature focus except for me. I was interested in the global economies and the politics of Scandinavia's membership in the European Union, so I split my time between the Scandinavian Studies and Political Science departments. This made me even more of an outsider from the beginning.

In my second semester of grad school, I made an important mental shift and decided to use my strengths in a new way within this environment. While the professors and other grad students knew far more than I did about the literature, I started challenging myself to speak up in every class to add a political perspective that wouldn't have been part of the conversation otherwise. When I spoke up, the conversation would take a different turn that was even more enriching for everyone around the table. With time, my professors seized the opportunity to pivot and explore our group conversations through the alternative lens on the assigned reading material. This then allowed me to see myself as a value-add rather than coming from a position of inferiority.

This is when I learned the value of bringing a fresh perspective rather than seeking out the comfort of simply fitting in or trying to confine my contributions by definition of a perfect score based around someone else's strengths rather than my own.

Forging Your Own Path

Before I left Seattle for California, I suspected I would miss the thrilling pace of Amazon, so, on my last day at Amazon, I emailed Udi Manber, president of A9, Amazon's search company based in Palo Alto, California. I asked Udi to let me know if he ever had special projects that could use my help or my specially trained think-like-Jeff skills. Udi replied right away, inviting me to visit him in nearby Palo Alto once I had settled in at Berkeley.

I agreed to work for him every Friday, managing special projects for the office of the president. While immersed in the all-encompassing academic environment of questioning and challenging the expert voices in the room, I was also diving headfirst into the intensely competitive world of Silicon Valley. The combination of the two felt like my perfect match. I was learning to trust my instincts, to be unafraid of questioning those superior to me, and to take a creative approach about what I wanted my days and work to be.

I was at my desk at A9 one Friday when my desk phone rang. As far as I knew, no one had my work number. *I* didn't even know the number. The person on the other end was a recruiter at Google named Jeff. He said that my name had come up from several sources and he was wondering if I was interested in exploring possible roles at Google. My immediate reaction was a firm no.

I had finally successfully navigated my way through my first bewildering year of my PhD curriculum. I was hitting my stride and contributing value to a program that had invested so much in my development. I felt loyalty to Berkeley, to my department, to the people in it—and to my dream of being a professor. I thanked Jeff for the kind offer but said that I was very happy in academics and wasn't interested in interviewing. I didn't even ask for his contact information before I hung up.

Jeff called me several times over the summer trying to convince me to come in for an interview. I politely declined again and again. While this was still the early years of Google, in 2006, he was probably not used to people telling him no. Google was already established as the coolest company in America to work for, and talented candidates were vying to get in.

On the fourth call, he asked me if I'd at least come to the Google campus for a tour and to meet some people. I had to admit that I was curious. I had heard the stories—about the free food, the volleyball courts, the wellness centers with on-site doctors, the massage rooms, the nap pods, and so on. You could bring your dog to work! I was curious to see how anyone got anything done in such an environment.

I went to Google and toured the campus, but what struck me most was the people I met there. They were some of the world's most interesting people working on fascinating and deeply technical projects. At lunch I found myself, by chance or by the recruiter's clever design, sitting between a former astronaut, a cyclist who had raced on the Postal Service team with Lance Armstrong in the Tour de France, and Vint Cerf, one of the founders of the internet.

This environment was in direct alignment with my ambitions. I could feel it.

My mind was buzzing. I had found my new home. I didn't feel one bit like an outsider despite the intimidating résumés around me. Something in me just knew that I belonged there.

At the end of the day, Jeff asked me what my biggest hesitation was for leaving academics. I told him that it had been a dream of mine to work with the smartest people in the world every day and to make a difference in the world. He couldn't stifle a laugh. "In *that* case," he said, "I think you'll be very happy here." He knew, and I knew, that I would be back.

Surround Yourself with Brilliance

The interview process at Google is intense. I started interviewing before I had decided I would accept an offer if they made one. At Google back in the early 2000s, even when you were recruited, you had to take an entrance exam before anyone would formally interview you. The exam was different for each department. Because I was being recruited for a position on the Product team, my exam was very similar to the part of the Law School Admission Test with brainteasers and complex problems. The test lasted several hours.

Historically I do not perform well on standardized tests. To my surprise, I got a perfect score. I'm not sure if the result was the effect of my sincerely being okay with the possibility of failure, because I wasn't yet certain I even wanted to leave my PhD studies, or if it was a demonstration of having learned complex problem-solving at Amazon. Either way, I felt completely at ease with the brainteasers presented, solving them, and explaining my solutions.

Because of my time working for Jeff Bezos, I was being recruited to be executive business partner to Marissa Mayer. At the time she was vice president of search products and user experience, on the Product team, in charge of the Google home page, doodles, maps, Gmail, news, and more. The Product team's job was to make useful tools and attract users to the services. It was up to other teams to figure out how best to monetize those products and services.

My first round of interviews was in Building 43 at Google headquarters in Mountain View. I was led through the lobby and up the large wooden staircase, above which hung a life-size replica of SpaceShipOne, winner of the Ansari X Prize less than two years before. The spaceship wasn't yet formally installed with the metal support beam; it hung above the stairs by what looked like a large leather belt, so low that you felt like you had to duck under it. Just outside of the main lobby was a replica of a *Tyrannosaurus rex* skeleton nicknamed Stan, molded from *T. rex* fossils of a dinosaur discovered near Google's headquarters. I sat in the conference room waiting for my interview with Marissa, taking in the unusual "decorations," and imagining myself working there. It was surprisingly easy to do so.

I wasn't surprised when Marissa arrived at my interview late. I'd already had phone interviews with her rescheduled three times. Her assistant had gone on emergency maternity leave due to complications, so Marissa's world was in a bit of chaos when we first met.

I liked her immediately. She had an easy, distinctive laugh—so distinctive that someone once made a ringtone out of it (which did not amuse her). She was sincere and warm. She was obviously extremely smart, was off-the-charts passionate about her work, and got straight to the point.

Many people, I would learn, were intimidated by her, but I didn't feel that way. She is as brilliant as she is tough and demanding when she needs to be. Her team members who interviewed me clearly respected her command of the room whether she was leading code reviews or digging into the details of a product design down to the individual pixel level. She was exhaustive in her pursuit of perfection and demanded the same of everyone on her team. Again, I felt an alignment of ambitions.

I had done my homework and read numerous articles about her, but I wanted to leave my mind open enough to form my own opinion, good or bad, in the interview. I had read every article I could find on her and felt that she was often judged harshly by others who felt intimidated by a brilliant, hard-charging woman who also happened to be beautiful; she wasn't the only woman in leadership who has had to deal with a whole other area of criticism that men never do.

I knew that working for her would not be easy, but it became apparent that I would learn a lot, and that is what sealed the deal for me. Marissa made it clear that she was on the path to becoming a CEO herself. (Several years later, she achieved her goal and became the CEO of Yahoo!.) I knew I wanted to be part of the team she was building. Google had grown astronomically in its few short years of existence. That year, Google doubled its number of employees from five thousand to ten thousand, and the company had an annual growth rate of over 87 percent. Everyone was working at a breakneck pace and seemed to be fueled by the shared adrenaline.

This team had already changed the way the world accessed information—and they were only getting started. The employees were unconventional and irreverent in their personal and thinking style; they were data-driven in their decision-making and goal-setting. The unapologetic pace, the audacious goals of the company, being a major player in inventing the future of technology . . . it was all intoxicating. I was swept up into this current and pulled far out to sea immediately. I knew there was no turning back.

The interviews happened in the summer of 2006. By the end of August, Google made me a formal offer. I tried to get hold of my professors and department chair at UC Berkeley to discuss this turn of events, but they were unreachable while on the summer break. I had several conversations with my parents about what to do, but they were rightfully neutral in their advice despite any leanings they harbored.

I hadn't changed my mind about wanting to be a professor. I loved my program and felt like I had finally had breakthrough moments, including a genuine understanding of what was expected in academics. I was sure the coming years would be even better and more rewarding.

The truth? My heart was clear, but my head wasn't ready to acknowledge it without a fight. After long deliberation, I accepted Google's offer. I kept the key to my office in my department's library on my key ring for the next ten years, a daily reminder that I could go back if this Google thing didn't work out. It was a needed comfort at times because my first few years at Google were far from easy.

FIND MEANINGFUL IMPACT

I had no idea that I would spend the next twelve years working at Google. I had even less of an indication that I would then leave the company to become the founder of an international consulting company with CEO clients all over the world. The things I have learned along the way changed the course of my life through seemingly small but constant pivots.

The number one differentiator in my life and career has been the absolute top quality of the people with and for whom I have worked. You don't have to work for a billionaire CEO or top tech company to have this up-leveling effect from your colleagues; however, you do need to be proactively cultivating it.

I always prioritized the type of people I wanted to work for over anything else, including the job title and salary, because I knew they would shape the kind of person and leader I would become. When I look at my peers who have found joy and impact in their work, I see that they have all sought out a team with the highest quality people who are smart, curious, kind, collaborative, and results-oriented.

Follow the Leader You Want to Become

The most consistent way I have up-leveled my career over the past two decades has been two part. First, I have prioritized finding a manager who is modeling the career path I want to take and embodies the leadership qualities I want to possess. Second, I have chosen roles that surround me with top-quality people and a depth of opportunities to grow with them. I could have stayed in roles that were easy for me and avoided the stress and discomfort that I experienced at these companies, but it would have come at the cost of my long-term growth and happiness.

I have learned that once most of my workday is spent in my comfort zone, my job becomes mundane and drains me of energy rather than refueling me with new knowledge and skills. I have consistently sought out new projects or roles when I am spending more than 80 percent of my time in my comfort zone every day. My next career steps have always been inspired by asking myself the key question of "What do I want to learn in the next phase of my career?" Without having a clear idea of what I want to learn, it's easy to unintentionally limit myself to roles and projects that won't bring my work to a new level through challenging and growing my skills.

I have never found myself in a situation where I felt my boss or my team wouldn't support my growth, but, if I did, I would like to think I would leave that job immediately. My past teams have driven me to take risks and achieve things I would have been too intimidated to attempt alone.

Looking back at my career path, it is obvious that my managers were often key indicators of the growth trajectory and opportunities available to me. They set the tone, pace, and milestones. My managers, whether CEOs or not, developed my talents by giving me growth opportunities and continually challenging me within a supportive environment. In exchange, it was up to me to be proactive with the opportunities. They were looking for results above all else, and I was determined to deliver.

Connecting the Opportunity Dots

In 2005 Steve Jobs gave the Stanford University commencement speech and shared a philosophy about growth and seizing opportunity that immediately resonated with me and made sense of my seemingly disjointed career choices. He said, "You can't connect the dots looking forward; you can only connect them looking backward. So you have to trust that the dots will somehow connect in your future. You have to trust in something—your gut, destiny, life, karma, whatever. This approach has never let me down, and it has made all the difference in my life." Deciding to make a dramatic career pivot to work for Google wasn't the first or the last time I would make a big bet in order to experience something that felt like a once-in-a-lifetime opportunity.

I have had the privilege of working at companies during periods of invention that will never happen again. To be at Amazon at the dawn of the internet and watch Jeff Bezos invent e-commerce is irreplicable. That moment in time will never happen again. To prepare myself for that role, I had to preface it with an unglamorous university job that taught me the core skills and gave me the confidence to try. The same pattern was true for my career at Google. I had the privilege to watch what is now one of the most powerful companies in the world move life-changing products from conception to launch to becoming indispensable parts of our lives.

My teams at Amazon and Google became like family to me. Not only did we spend more hours together than we did with our actual families, but our experiences together shaped me in significant ways. It pains me when I meet people who hate their jobs. I have a lot of friends across the globe who haven't been able to find a role that provides the challenges and opportunities for the advancement they crave because of lack of local opportunities. I am happy to see the internet starting to level this playing field and providing a more global economy of opportunity, but there is still a long way to go. It can still feel like working in an industry that brings personal fulfillment is an unattainable luxury that is only available to the elite because those types of careers, education, and technology might not be available in a particular city. It is my personal quest to help overcome these barriers of entry for everyone.

A lot of life's wear and tear around work can often be offset by purposefully choosing to surround ourselves with people to lift us up and inspire us to be and do more. In the early stages of my career, when inspiring people were not available within my work environment, it was even more vital for me to seek them out in my personal life and spend as much time together collaborating on as many fulfilling projects as possible.

Sometimes luck is not on our side and we have to take a job that in no way resembles our dream job or desired career path in order to pay our bills. Don't despair. This is a natural part of *all* careers, no matter how glamorous they appear on the outside, and there are ways to create growth opportunities even in these less-than-ideal roles. Sara Blakely, the self-made billionaire founder of Spanx, sold fax machines door-to-door for seven years and credits the massive success of her company to the core sales skills and the ability to not be dissuaded by rejection that she learned in those years. Any job, no matter how mundane, can teach us core skills that can drive the dream careers of our future.

The key to seemingly impossible breakthrough success is being unafraid of starting small. Just about everyone likes the idea of being a celebrity CEO, but not many of us are willing to trade in absolutely everything we have to build something alone in our garage. Starting small can be your greatest advantage, so don't apologize for it or discount this stage as unimportant.

My first jobs could have been very ordinary and not impactful. I was "just" an office manager, then "just" an assistant, then "just" the junior-most academic in my PhD program. However, with a little resourcefulness, I created opportunities out of seemingly nothing that became career-changing moments. So can you!

Make the Ordinary Extraordinary

If someone had asked me what my dream was when I started my very first job, it would in no way resemble the career that I've had or the path on which I now find myself. I never intended to work in tech, let alone for the CEOs of two of the most disruptive companies in history. In fact, I was always jealous of those who knew their life's goal from an early age. I've discovered that just wasn't the case for me—or for most people. The key was that I did know what I wanted to *learn* in my life, even if I didn't know what exactly I wanted to *do*.

I remember at a very young age wanting so badly to be special, to be the best in the world at something—anything!

Unfortunately, I wasn't born with incredible talent. Fortunately, I learned that passion, purpose, and being great at something doesn't only arrive with your DNA. They are things you can cultivate and develop over time. The legendary designer Diane von Furstenberg once said, "I didn't know what I wanted to do, but I always knew the woman I wanted to be."

Life's greatest joys follow once you have a dream so strong that it pulls you forward, rather than the other way around.

Are you the hero of your own dreams? Early in my career, back in 2002, I was at Jeff Bezos's home early one morning helping to prepare for a senior strategy session with the S-Team, his senior leadership team. As Jeff and our team were setting up his boathouse for the meeting, he told us about his dream the previous night, where he had to save the human race from unknown alien attackers. His then wife, MacKenzie, chimed in that one of the things she admired most about Jeff was that he was always the hero in his own dreams. How different, I thought, from my own dreams. Often in my nightmares I would be unable to run or powerless even to scream. Not Jeff. He was the hero.

Over the three years I spent working at his side, I learned from Jeff the keys to empowering yourself to be the hero of your own dreams and overcome growth paralysis. I am lucky to have learned many empowering lessons from legendary leaders. The common denominator of their insights on how to accomplish your wildest dreams is to realize that you are the designer of your own fate, and you are the person you were meant to be.

CHAPTER 2 ROI SPRINT

Amazing things happen when we are willing to pivot and trust our instincts enough to take a chance on an opportunity that might never come our way again. Are you ready to place a serious bet on a dream career and life? Are you ready to create a tribe of brilliant and inspiring people who will help you forge your own path rather than follow one that is easy yet unfulfilling? Where can you spend time with leaders you want to emulate? What are the ways in which you can take some risks to exchange your ordinary for the extraordinary?

Recognize: Are you at a stage in your career where your daily tasks and opportunities fall below your ambition? Are you surrounded by people you want to emulate? Are there irreplicable growth opportunities around you that you haven't taken a chance on out of fear? What kinds of projects make you spring out of bed in the morning? What is the common denominator, and how can you invite more of this into your work and life?

Own: What do you need to change in order to align yourself in your work with what motivates you most? Whose buy-in can you get today on a plan to make this shift? How can you create opportunities within your current network that align with your growth goals and expose you to stellar people?

Implement: Take the steps necessary to start learning the skills you value most and gaining the experiences you crave today!

INCREASING YOUR IMPACT

*B*uilding resilience is the single greatest skill needed to survive in innovative and competitive environments and anytime you are making a bet on yourself and leveling up. Luck might have got my foot in the door a few critical times in my career, but resilience allowed me not only to take steps inside the rooms where core decisions were being made but also to drag in my own chair and take a seat at the table.

Let me tell you, there were a lot of missteps and tumbles along the way. However, those strategic challenges—much more than your successes—are the way you gain respect and grow at the upper limits of your abilities. As much as I prefer to avoid embarrassment and struggle, I don't think that this step is skippable.

I have worked with and known more than my fair share of billionaires and highly successful people, and every single one of them, without exception, has incredible resilience. This is not by chance. They have gained this through constant trial and error, occasionally humiliating mistakes, scrutiny under blinding spotlights, and purposely building their dreams one brick at a time over and over again.

I can tell you from personal experience that despite their CEO celebrity personas, they absolutely feel the weight of their mistakes and the pain of disappointing results. They haven't succeeded because they avoided mistakes; in fact, they invited them because that is where the most learning lies. What differentiates them is that they ran toward the potential for failure, and when they stumbled, they did not stay down for long. What fuels this incredible resilience is their larger purpose and mission.

The keys to this level of resilience are:

- Accelerated learning through failure
- Mastering the quick pivot
- Calculated risk-taking

My CEO managers taught me that resilience is a natural result of being aligned with a mission greater than yourself. This is what fuels your ability to make mistakes over and over again as you inch your way closer to your ideal. Jeff Bezos regularly said that entrepreneurs need to be willing to be misunderstood for a very long time. This takes an incredible amount of resilience.

I have had to learn to tolerate risk and potential embarrassment in order to accomplish my goals in life. Had I not done so, my life would have remained small and unfulfilling. Thankfully my career forced me to learn quickly that if I had any hope of accomplishing what I valued most in life, being of service to as many people as possible, that I had to choose bravery. To be honest, it might be more accurate to say that I chose resilience and the bravery followed.

ACCELERATED LEARNING
THROUGH FAILURE

As mentioned at the beginning of this book, I once almost killed Jeff Bezos.

A few months after I started at Amazon, Jeff stopped by my desk with an unusual project. There were properties in Texas he wanted to visit, and he had only a short window of a few days in which to do so. He cryptically placed a slip of paper that had on it several long series of numbers on my desk. At first, I wondered if this was another brainteaser, but then—as the daughter of a former fighter pilot—I realized what the numbers were: GPS coordinates.

Soon enough I had made a map of the locations, but I also realized that they were too far apart to drive to in the limited time Jeff had allotted. Using the chartered jet wouldn't work, either, because the airports near the properties were spaced such that it would also waste too much time.

I took my findings to my manager, John. "I don't think what Jeff wants is possible," I told him. "We either need more time, or we need to narrow the list of the properties he wants to visit."

I had barely gotten the last word of my assessment out of my mouth when John replied, "No is not an answer."

I went back to my desk and pondered. I thought about the problem, and I eventually figured out that the ideal transportation had to be faster than a car and less complicated to start and stop than a plane.

A helicopter!

Excitedly, I told John of my idea.

"Good, do that!" he said without looking up, as if hiring a helicopter was a simple, normal task.

I was in my early twenties and had never hired a helicopter. I certainly didn't have helicopter-related contacts in my Rolodex. I thought for a while and decided to reach out to the jet charter company we were using for the charter flight from Seattle to Texas to see if I could book a helicopter through them. Success!

The Value of Rock Bottom

I completed the security screening with our in-house team and booked my first helicopter. To my great relief, the trip went smoothly and Jeff returned from Texas with increased enthusiasm about his project. (I had no idea yet what he had in mind to build there.) A few weeks later, Jeff asked me to book another trip to Texas. He wanted one more look at his new favorite properties before making a decision on which to buy.

Jeff and his pilot were off on the adventure, scheduled to return the next day. But then something happened that burned every second of that trip to Texas into my brain and each nerve in my body. In my mind I can see it play frame by frame, in excruciating slow motion.

That morning I had come into the office early, as usual, preparing for the day. I was reading a briefing document when my desk phone rang. It was one of the jet pilots. I had never received a call from the crew before. They told me not to be alarmed, which of course made me instantly alarmed. They were preparing the paperwork for the return flight from Texas to Seattle the next day when they had heard an emergency beacon go off on the scanner.

They couldn't confirm that it was Jeff's helicopter, or what had happened to the helicopter in question, but chances were not small that it was his and that it had crashed.

My hands started shaking, and I couldn't hold a pen steady enough to write. I called my manager, John, and he agreed with my idea to call an emergency board meeting to prepare for all possible scenarios. We needed to be prepared with a communication and strategy plan in case Jeff was, in fact, injured or dead. I knew that it would take some time for the distress call of the helicopter in question to be answered by emergency crews, since its location was not close to any major cities or hospitals.

All I could think about was how I might have killed Jeff Bezos, as well as the entire Amazon company, and maybe the future of online commerce. At that point, in early 2003, virtually the entire value of Amazon was based on faith in Jeff. The company was not yet "truly" profitable. Amazon had had profitable quarters, but for the first five years of the company's growth, Jeff purposely didn't focus on profitability.

Under Jeff's visionary leadership, Amazon was one of the sole surviving tech companies of the dot-com bust. That experience fed Jeff's instincts to be frugal, yet unapologetically bold in his growth strategy, and to follow an unconventional business plan despite the doubts of his investors. I feared that all of that brilliant strategy and those countless years of hard work by Jeff and everyone at Amazon might now be gone with the crash of a helicopter somewhere in the middle of West Texas.

A few long hours later, I learned that the helicopter I had hired for Jeff Bezos, one of the greatest visionaries of the modern age, *did* crash, with him inside, but no one knew exactly where the helicopter was or the fate of its passengers.

While we assembled the emergency board meeting to prepare a game plan for all possible scenarios, I started calling hospitals in the far western Texas counties, asking if anyone had been brought in from a helicopter crash. The first few calls were met with confused responses. Then, finally, at the fourth hospital I called, the receptionist responded to my question by asking, "Are you family?" I knew I had found him.

Jeff had been visiting a ranch in a canyon near Cathedral Mountain, Texas. The day had started out cool, and the single-engine helicopter took off with Jeff, his personal assistant, and the pilot on board. They flew to the first ranch Jeff wanted to see (again) and picked up the ranch owner, a particularly large man, to do an aerial survey of the property. By this time the air had warmed, and the engine wasn't powerful enough for the additional weight on board. Upon takeoff, the tail of the helicopter clipped a tree, and the helicopter flipped upside down and crashed into a nearby creek, splitting open like a broken egg.

Jeff proved himself a superhero that day, truly. I have a feeling he enjoys telling this story (who wouldn't?) because he saved everyone on board. (Meanwhile, I still get sweaty palms every time I think about that day.)

When the helicopter crashed into the creek, Jeff pulled himself free, then promptly did the same for the pilot. He then pulled the ranch owner, whose shoulder was badly injured, off of his personal assistant, who had cracked a vertebrae in her back and was trapped under the ranch owner. Once everyone was safe, Jeff used the satellite phone I packed for him to call for help and get everyone medevacked to the nearest hospital.

The day of the crash was the first day of work for Amazon's new vice president of communications, so she had a memorable start to her company tenure. By the time Jeff called in to the board of directors, they had already drafted announcements for multiple scenarios, including his death.

Jeff told the board not to issue any proactive statements and to bury the story as much as possible. What no one but Jeff knew at the time was that he was buying property in Texas to build what would become Blue Origin, his private space-tourism company.

Going to space had been a dream of Jeff's since he was a small boy. He was five years old when Neil Armstrong did the first moon walk, and that made a huge impression on him. In his valedictorian speech upon graduating from high school, he told his classmates that he would go to space—not that he *wanted* to go to space; that he *would*. Building Blue Origin was to be the fulfillment of that commitment. He was going to compete for the newly founded XPrize for private space flight. Jeff, his dream, and the future of Amazon almost died that day.

I was prepared to be fired. I figured that almost killing your CEO boss is grounds for dismissal. However, when Jeff talked to me after the accident, he said some of the most cherished words I've ever heard: "Ann," he said, "I hear you're really good under pressure." I have never been more relieved or grateful in my life.

Confidence to Get Back Up

That moment changed our working relationship and my mindset, forever. Jeff now had the confidence that I, a junior employee, could be trusted with major responsibilities, to keep calm, and to ask the right questions, especially if things go horribly wrong. Perhaps more importantly, I learned to trust myself and my instincts even in the face of possible catastrophe.

The worst day of my professional life taught me how much failure can accelerate your learning. Had that helicopter not crashed, I think it would have taken me years to learn everything I did on that single day about trusting my instincts, managing a crisis, delegating, communicating with people very senior to me, and leading without official authority.

I will never say that I'm glad the helicopter crashed. But I'm eternally grateful for what it taught me about myself. Also: From that moment on, I would only hire helicopters with two engines!

Thankfully for me, coming back from near disaster was a regular part of the Amazon experience. Jeff himself had been *Time* magazine's Person of the Year in 1999. At the age of thirty-five, he was the fourth youngest person to have this honor—only behind aviator Charles Lindbergh (who was twenty-five and the first to receive the award), Queen Elizabeth at age twenty-six, and Martin Luther King Jr. at thirty-four. But after this honor, things took a downward turn for Amazon, and it would take four years for Jeff to come back from it.

At the time, Amazon was only in its fourth year and was not yet profitable. It had grown from just three hundred customers in 1995 to over thirteen million customers and $8 billion in sales in 1999. Despite this success, Wall Street was still skeptical if Amazon would ever turn a profit, and they feared that it would become a victim of the dot-com crash. Despite the lack of profit, Amazon continued to have a high valuation.

By 2000, Jeff had borrowed $2 billion to keep the company going, as the dot-com bust approached. By the time I joined Amazon in 2002, the company had narrowly avoided bankruptcy, but 14 percent of the distribution-center employees were laid off when revenues stagnated.

In my second year, 2003, the company rebounded, as Jeff's long-term growth strategy took root, and Amazon turned a $400 million profit. This was followed by a steady increase and then, of course, the astronomical growth we continue to see today, thanks to Jeff's big bets and determination to succeed.

Jeff was confident in his plan despite the skeptics. He led our team and company into projects that created and shaped what is now modern e-commerce. He insisted on focusing on long-term growth rather than being tempted to make short-term profit decisions to appease investors, as some competitors had done, and that ended up making all the difference in creating the dominant company that Amazon is today. But the full effects were far in the future at the time, and skeptics started to wonder if Jeff, too, would fail.

Jeff's vision and all of our hard work started to pay off at the end of 2003, and we announced Amazon's first profitable year. The company expanded rapidly into new markets and new products beyond books. In my first year at Amazon, in 2002, Jeff had launched Super Saver Shipping, which is nowadays a staple for most consumers, something we can hardly imagine living without.

Despite the eventual massive success of that innovation, the board of directors was initially unconvinced that it would work. They were doubtful that it was a sustainable business plan, given Amazon's already-modest profit margin and Jeff's unconventional business model. I hovered around those early board meetings and heard discussions of bringing in a "professional CEO" with more experience, to keep these seemingly crazy Bezos ideas in check.

Jeff learned a lot about himself during those early years while consistently on the brink of failure. He became risk tolerant, hired only people who would raise the bar, invested heavily in the user experience, and made big, unapologetic bets on himself. He is the best example I can give of someone who has used failure to his long-term advantage because he was willing to see failure as accelerated learning.

MASTERING THE QUICK PIVOT

You learn a lot about yourself and your colleagues when you almost kill your boss. That early lesson of resilience was vital for me to learn in order to have a successful career in Silicon Valley. Many years later, that resilience muscle would need to be flexed again after failing early in my new role at Google. It is easy to make errors of omission when you are so distracted with overwhelm that you forget what you are trying to build in the first place.

My first five years at Google were extremely challenging, for several reasons. My first year was difficult because of the steep learning curve and avalanche of work that was immediately thrown on top of me, with little to no guidance given on how to accomplish any of it.

The team was on tight deadlines and was challenged with innovating, implementing, and delivering products at a breakneck pace. There was no time to breathe let alone time for anyone to explain to me what the names, acronyms, and technical terms they threw around meant. Nowadays when someone starts at Google, there is literally an internal reference dictionary available to you so that you can learn the Google lingo. Back then, I was completely on my own.

When I started, I didn't know anyone and had no resources to complete the tasks that were given to me. At that stage of the company, there were few documented procedures for how to do anything. You just made it up as you went, tried to do the right thing, gathered the essential decision makers, and hoped that it worked. Everything was done through relationships because the company was still small enough that you could know almost everyone by name. Unfortunately for me, I started out knowing no one and was tasked with huge projects that were already behind schedule.

Pick Your Head Up

My very first day at Google was actually a team off-site in a nearby hotel conference room. Marissa's entire Search Products team was packed into the room, and they each took turns presenting their idea for what Google products could be in ten years' time. Some of the presentations were hand-drawn sketches while some were formal mockups. The quality of the presentation style didn't matter at all. The entire exercise was about challenging yourself to imagine the needs of Google users in the future and how we could build the technology and tools today that would eventually be needed. This was the future-looking-back approach to product vision that makes Google the force it is today.

The only presentation I remember specifically was an early idea of what later became Google image search, which we now use every day. It was a radical idea for the time to be able to offer search results with image-recognition technology that hadn't yet been invented. It was very complex and involved indexing inconceivable amounts of visual data, and it took years to accomplish. I was watching history being made from day one.

Despite these glimpses of greatness and the thrill of the company mission, my day-to-day tasks in that first year at Google were mostly thankless, invisible, and never-ending. My instinct was to deal with my overwhelming workload by digging in and working eighteen-hour days, trying to play catch-up to a backlog that preceded me. This was a disastrous approach.

I still have my notebook from that first year, and it is full of frenzied, barely legible notes that are largely questions to myself about what my assignments even meant (because everything in a project was referred to by code names that meant nothing to me), who I was supposed to collaborate with (because most employees were referred to by their email handle—or LDAP—rather than their actual names), and what the deadline actually was (because each launch date depended on the fate of several other simultaneous projects with evolving timelines).

I shared an office with Marissa and two of her other direct reports. Our office was the hub of action on campus. Most days it seemed like every single member of the seven hundred–person Product team cycled through our office at least once. I learned to tune out most of the chaos and only tune in to the chaos that involved me.

I almost never left my desk. There was a café less than a minute's walk from my desk that served incredible free meals three times a day that I never visited. I was too busy to eat. When colleagues would get worried and bring me food, I would forget it was sitting there next to my keyboard for hours and then eventually have to guiltily throw it out. I remember fearing I'd get a bladder infection from never getting up to go to the restroom that was less than ten feet from my desk. I was overwhelmed.

After a few months, something finally broke. I remember actually feeling pretty good that day. I was finally feeling part of the team and like I understood what we were building and what needed to get done. I had made a few friends who were amazing people and helped me learn the lingo and how to get things done. But then Marissa was acting really weird. She was normally really talkative and energetic, and that day she was quiet, when I saw her at all. It was like she was really angry with me and avoiding me but I couldn't think of a single reason why she should be.

I tried to ignore the feeling, but by the end of the day, after her avoiding my attempts to talk, I followed her out to her car. We had developed what I thought was a good working relationship, so I pushed her when she said that everything was fine. When I pressed again, the truth spilled out.

There was a big meeting with the CEO, Eric Schmidt, and all of the senior vice presidents the next day that Marissa hadn't been told about but was meant to attend. His assistant had forgotten to add Marissa to the calendar entry, since she was the only non-SVP on the list and was not included in the usual group alias. Marissa had conflicting personal plans, a very rare occurrence, which she absolutely could not change because people were already on planes flying in from around the country for the event, but that didn't feel like a reasonable reason to miss the meeting with our CEO.

And Marissa was mad at *me*. She was far more upset about the fact that I didn't know about the meeting than she was about the fact that the CEO's assistant had forgotten to invite her.

I was heartbroken. It felt unfair and personal. I made a list in my head of all of the sacrifices I had made for this job. I had left my PhD program to work eighteen-hour days to help her and the entire Product team be successful in launching their work into the world, and now this was the thanks I got in return?

I sulked on the hour-and-a-half-long Google shuttle ride home rather than reading my work emails as I normally did. As I lay awake in bed that night, I finally had a moment of clarity. I decided that she was actually right. I had been stuck in a performance mindset and hadn't lifted my eyes above the overwhelming number of tasks piled on my desk from my first day. I had forgotten that, as her executive business partner, I was there to represent her and the team's best interests. The other tasks, while important, were secondary. It was a mistake of omission, but, intentional or not, I had failed.

In that moment of sleeplessness, I decided to make an immediate pivot.

Work Smarter, Not Harder

In order to do my job effectively, I needed to raise my sights and focus on what was needed for me to produce success for Marissa and my team: relationships. I needed to get up from my desk, create new connections, and not worry about the smaller tasks piling up. If relationships were the way to get things done at Google, then I needed to build up what I came to refer to as my reserve of "friendship currency" in the company.

I needed to create a network of trust, do some favors, and make people want to work with me. Had I done this earlier, the CEO's assistant wouldn't have forgotten to invite Marissa because she would have realized her mistake in advance when she saw my face in the café or heard my name from another connection. I had been working very hard but not very smart. It was time for a change. I started to prioritize and proactively create opportunities to bond with my colleagues and build up relationships.

There is an analogy about rocks, pebbles, and sand that illustrates this learning well and that was popularized by Stephen Covey, the author of *The 7 Habits of Highly Effective People*. The analogy talks about filling a jar, starting with rocks, then pebbles, and finally sand, which fills in any remaining gaps. The rocks represent your major milestone goals, the pebbles are the tasks surrounding the shorter-term goals, and the grains of sand are the minor tasks that never seem to go away but that aren't what drive success. If you put the sand in the jar first, there is no room for the essential rocks. This is a common mistake among junior employees, and I was no exception. The order of execution is an essential part of the formula for success.

It is possible to work really hard on smaller, often easier, "sand"-level tasks and not be any closer to success. I learned the vital lesson to focus my attention, energy, and time solely on moving the "rocks" that were the foundation of our future successes and to trust that the other parts would fill in around them.

This was a breakthrough realization for me and a major pivot point right at the beginning of what became a twelve-year career at Google, and it definitely wasn't my last. I would fail to identify core rocks and then need to pivot constantly, and that pattern led to ultimate success.

CALCULATED RISK-TAKING

My relationship with Marissa improved significantly, and I really enjoyed our partnership. I was both thrilled and terrified when she asked me to join her on a trip with the senior leadership to a conference in Zurich. This seemed like the perfect opportunity to get to know more of the team and get involved in the impactful, global projects they were focused on.

We all flew together on the Google founders' private 757 from California to Zurich, with about twenty members of the Google leadership on board. I had never been on a private flight before, let alone in a private 757, surrounded by some of the most influential people in the world.

I remember being very nervous and unsure of what was expected of me. About an hour into the flight, I was working on my laptop while sitting in a chair toward the back of the plane, just trying to stay out of the way, when Larry Page, Google's cofounder, walked over to me and asked me a question. Even though Larry's office was just a few steps down the hall from mine and we saw each other every day, we had never chatted socially before. I was thrilled at the chance to talk and get to know him better, and I was nervous to make a good impression.

I stood up to talk to him and placed my open laptop on my seat. As Larry and I were talking, the flight attendant brought over a Diet Coke for me that I had forgotten she had offered. Then, suddenly, there was a huge bump of turbulence, and Larry and I both lost our balance and nearly fell over. The Diet Coke flew out of my hand, and the full glass poured out all over my open laptop keyboard and the light-gray fabric of my seat.

I was mortified. Not only had I destroyed company equipment and stained the seat on a private jet, but Larry had watched me do it. I wanted to just open the plane door and throw myself out.

Larry was unfazed and kindly said to me, "They're only things. We can fix that. At least you're okay!" Despite his sincere kindness, I felt horrible. While everyone else eventually fell asleep on the flight and stretched out across chairs, sofas, and the floor, I just sat upright, awake, staring at my laptop, which would not turn on, and feeling sick about what had happened.

I allowed myself to wallow in humiliation for the duration of the flight and then decided that I had better change my attitude. I could allow this "sand"-level failure to humiliate me and hold me back, or I could make up for it by being even more productive and useful for the rest of the trip. When we arrived at the Google Zurich office, I ran to the TechStop and had them issue me a new laptop and then joined our executive team at the conference.

Leading from Behind

I didn't sleep much for the next three days because of jet lag and my guilt-fueled drive to contribute as much value as possible. I made the most out of every second and took opportunities to bond with the senior leadership in a more personal way than we had had the opportunity to do while at headquarters in Mountain View, California. Marissa and I also got some valuable one-on-one time on our last night in Zurich when she took me for fondue at a restaurant that had been her favorite spot when she interned at the nearby UBS's research lab just after she had graduated from Stanford and before joining Google.

At the end of the trip, Marissa told me how helpful it was to have me there and that I had done a great job. I was so glad I was able to refocus myself and use that humiliation as motivation rather than being tempted to shrink into the background.

That skill has come in handy many times over my career while enduring several embarrassing failures in front of very important people. Without my pivot at the beginning of that trip, I never would have built the relationships with the top executives in the company that later led to me being trusted with the high-level projects and assignments that came my way over the next nine years.

Having the wisdom to make quick pivots after failure is what makes the difference between earning trust and being overlooked for projects and promotions. This is why Google emphasizes "failing early and often," because this kind of growth is only possible when you fully embrace this learning cycle and apply the lessons immediately.

The most effective way I've found to become indispensable and stand out on a team, especially early in my career, has been to consistently be the one who is willing to do the things that no one else wants to do, especially if you haven't been asked. This is how you build a reputation of always getting the right things done, for having a strong vision and insight, and for being a proactive player. This has been the core to every one of my promotions and recruitments.

Choosing the right risks to take is at the core of all innovation and breakthrough transformations and is especially important in our individual career-growth strategies.

I worked for Marissa Mayer on the Product team for three years, and I saw risk-taking in action every single day. It was a time full of challenges, adventures, heartaches, and forming lifelong memories. To this day, most of my closest friendships stem from those early years at Google. There is something special about enduring historic hardships together that forms lasting bonds.

Under Marissa's leadership I learned how to motivate a huge team to pivot in sync, consistently generate new ideas, and hit our targets. I also gained an essential understanding of how to get things done in the company and the way in which you can take an idea from conception to launch. This is almost never a smooth, linear production process. There are always unexpected hurdles. I came to appreciate every stage in that creation cycle and every person's role in the production line. This foundational knowledge was key for the next chapter in my career.

Some risk-taking is done in teams, and some risks we have to take alone. Sometimes individual advancement can make others around us feel threatened.

Upsetting the Status Quo

One day Eric Schmidt's executive assistant, Pam, came to me to say that there was an opening in the CEO's office, and they wanted to know if I was interested in joining his team. I had interacted with them before around various product launches but really only knew the team peripherally.

I liked Pam's leadership style and spunk. She was the self-proclaimed "Mama Duck" of the company and kept everyone lovingly in line and in sync. She had worked with Eric in three companies at which he had been CEO over the previous decade, and they had an amazing working relationship. I hadn't even considered making a move from Marissa's team and initially struggled with how to respond. In the end, my curiosity won over, and I decided there was no harm in having a conversation and learning more about the role and what it might be like working with Eric.

I had seen the way in which Eric Schmidt, the Google CEO, recruited his senior executives with careful attention to their unique talents, goals, and drive. I had heard the stories about how he closed the deal to hire Sheryl Sandberg, who had been concerned about the parameters of her role should she come on board. Google, even to this day, hires for talent rather than focusing on a specific open role to be filled. Many candidates are hired before they even know what they will be working on. Sheryl had been concerned about this unorthodox hiring approach and wanted to know more about what exactly she would be contributing by joining. Eric's final sales pitch was to tell her that when you are offered a ride on a rocket ship, you don't stop to ask which seat; you just get on. Sheryl accepted the offer. And so did I.

In my informal interview with Eric, he thankfully didn't ask me any brainteasers as Jeff Bezos had years before. Eric said that my past résumé at Amazon and performance at Google were proof enough that I had the right skills for the job and all we needed to know was if he and I were a good fit as teammates. I was a little surprised that Eric even knew who I was, let alone that he knew of my reputation. I have to admit it made those seemingly invisible tasks and thankless long nights over the previous three years feel even more worth the effort.

I immediately liked the way Eric described his work philosophy in long-term goals and with an eye to not only impact but also legacy building. He prioritized having a stellar team around him in order to accomplish his professional goals, so he proactively sought out the best talent available. I felt honored and compelled to say yes when he offered me the job in that meeting.

This career move was one of the most impactful of my life, but it came at the price of several years of awkwardness that I had not anticipated. The first came from Marissa taking personal offense at my decision to move to the CEO's team. She took my departure as a gesture of my lack of faith in her career trajectory and goals to become a CEO herself. That couldn't have been further from the truth. I was absolutely certain that she would be CEO one day soon, and I had fully anticipated being part of that journey with her.

The truth was that Eric had won me over when he described his philosophy around how he builds his teams. He said that he approaches his work like running a marathon. He invests in building up strength and stamina in the people around him. He invests time in them, gives them challenging projects at the edge of their abilities, and gives them full autonomy to learn, experiment, and grow. Marissa, too, invested deeply in developing and supporting her team. She consistently fought hard for our compensation, progression, and recognition. However, Eric was able to offer a team environment with more extensive resources and built-in backup, which meant I would no longer feel the pressure of being a single point of failure for an entire team as an individual contributor.

Working for Marissa had been a daily thrill of attempting to sprint a marathon, but my runner's high was wearing off. I had attempted to implement several systems with her in order to build in some pacing and efficiencies that would allow us to work smarter and not just harder. But the truth is that Marissa is one of those superhumans who does not need sleep or outside reju-venation like the rest of us in order to perform miraculous feats of professional strength. She wasn't living in denial, but it turns out that I was.

My personal life was taking a turn for the worse, and I needed a more sustainable pace that still offered me once-in-a-lifetime projects and opportunities for impact. And that combination was only possible with this career move and by being on a team again.

I also had to recognize that I didn't want to be held back by the fear of disappointing someone, and I needed to choose the right opportunities for advancement for myself. It was a risk worth taking. I didn't want to be overlooked for project leadership and promotions in the future by not being willing to take calculated steps toward learning core skills and building up my expertise in other parts of the company.

I knew that I needed to have a solid growth plan and enlist buy-in and help along the way from key stakeholders. I knew that this new role would lead to projects that otherwise I wouldn't have been involved in. This was not a passive decision, and I invited judgment and scrutiny from people whose opinions I highly valued, but I took the risk that it would be worth the reward. I felt like this was the best way for me to rise through the ranks at Google and get noticed. In order to do this, I had to get comfortable with being uncomfortable for a long time.

The truth is that this same pattern of disappointing an executive with my career decisions had happened with Jeff Bezos as well. A few years after I left Amazon, a former colleague was traveling with Jeff for a conference in California, so we got together to catch up after work. I had been thrilled to see him and hear how all of my friends were doing and about how the company was really booming. My joy went sour when he shared with me that Jeff had been upset when he heard that I had left my PhD to work at Google, which he considered a competitor. At first I was just baffled that Jeff was talking or thinking about me at all, but then it really stung. To this day it pulls at my heart to think that he somehow might have personalized my career decision in a way that made him feel like it was a slight to him and what we had built as a team both at Amazon and at A9.

The common denominator is that for leaders like Jeff Bezos and Marissa Mayer, their work and their person are one and the same. They are defined by what they do and those who follow them. That is why they are amazing at what they are able to accomplish. I consider both of them to be an essential part of my professional family and history, regardless of how they felt in a moment of seeming betrayal.

I had to actively put together a plan for reclaiming my confidence through purposeful growth rather than allowing myself to wallow in the discomfort of disappointing people I respected. And that wasn't the only way in which this career change forced me to become comfortable being uncomfortable.

Sit at the Core Center of Growth

During this period of change in my career, I was suddenly freed up from any existing expectations of what my role or methods should look like. I shifted my sights from my peer level and refocused on opportunities for larger growth and impact.

I set two very important goals for myself that first quarter working for Eric. The first was to have all of the senior vice presidents and members of the board of directors get to know me and trust me. The second was to understand the core growth strategy of the company inside and out.

I knew that if I was going to have the impact I wanted to have from moving into the C-suite at Google, I would need to find a way to partner with people very senior to me and gain their trust and respect. It took me a while to figure out how to accomplish the first phase of these goals.

Every Monday Eric had his senior staff meeting with the founders and senior vice presidents of Google. The submissions and materials for this meeting were due on Fridays so that the agenda could be finalized and people could review the materials and prepare over the weekend. All of the submitted materials were assembled into a single packet. Inevitably these materials were submitted over the weekend, rather than on Friday, because of the growing volume of information needing to be reported and the nature of some of the financial reports, which couldn't be analyzed before the week's end. In this problem I saw an opportunity to meet my personal goals and contribute something of value to the most senior members of the company.

These packets were assembled by a project manager, Yael, with whom I had worked while on the Product team. I volunteered to help her chase down the missing submissions every week and assemble the final packets by Monday morning, which meant that I would be working every weekend.

While I didn't love working weekends, I did value having the SVPs and their teams in regular contact with me. We worked hard together, and we created vital relationships. I got to know what every part of the company was working on, what was going well, the areas in which the teams were struggling, and the places the company was dedicating resources for strategic growth.

Working on this project gave me unparalleled access to the inner workings of the company during a time of particularly vital growth. Poring over every report also helped me in my other responsibilities because this information informed my recommendations and ability to provide helpful feedback and guidance. I started to see trends and know when a team or product launch was about to be successful or when it needed special attention and resources to prevent disasters.

In order to get to that point, I had to ask a lot of questions, which exposed my lack of knowledge about several key areas of the company. I absolutely hate asking dumb questions, but I knew there was no other way. I could not fake my way through it and still accomplish my larger goal. I had to get comfortable allowing the most powerful people in the company to see me uncomfortable as I filled in my knowledge gaps. I had learned to lean into this feeling in graduate school, when I often felt like the extreme novice among experts. It was a calculated risk.

The need for uncomfortable risk-taking did not end with the passing of time as I had expected. And likely that is what kept me at Google for twelve years. The habit of volunteering for things outside of my core skills and job description that I'd started during my early years at the company only accelerated as I grew more and more comfortable in my work.

Over the decade working for Eric, I committed myself more and more to increase my contributions on the strategy and content side. To allow my ambitions to scale without working myself to death, I had to be creative in streamlining processes, delegating tasks, and bringing in new partners and practices so I could free up time to focus on new challenges. It took some time to get it right, and there were some awkward moments along the way as we all adjusted.

The truth is that these moments of self-doubt when taking a risk never fully go away regardless of how senior or experienced you become. If you are learning and growing, you are experiencing this kind of discomfort daily. The goal is to never spend too much time in your comfort zone. All effective leaders have done the hard work in building up their confidence and skills and have learned how to take calculated risks to push themselves and their new ideas forward.

This sets the stage for what entrepreneurs call "moonshot projects." This is how the founders of all of the major, disruptive tech companies created their vision. This is a future-looking-back way of approaching challenges.

Moonshots, by nature, are projects so lofty and complicated that failures along the way are guaranteed. Before undertaking a moonshot, you have to have learned to make the right bets, not fear failure, how to pivot and draw creatively on your resources, and how to apply your learnings to forge a stronger path forward. It is for this reason that venture capitalists in Silicon Valley often prefer to invest in founders with multiple failed ventures in their past, because without these experiences, entrepreneurs lack the wisdom, confidence, and other tools to be successful in moonshot projects. For these expert investors, past failures are not a detriment but an essential predictor of future success. The people who have failed have built up the resilience necessary for the path to huge impact.

Shouldn't we view ourselves the same way? Moonshots happen when we contribute to our larger community by building something larger than ourselves. It's a thrilling idea to build something that will live on beyond you!

Staying firmly within our comfort zones might feel like the safer, less risky option. But the truth is that this in and of itself is a failure—failure to reach your potential and failure to experience the joy and learning that would otherwise be available to you.

Any meaningful success comes only after repeating the cycle of choosing the right bet, experimenting, failing, pivoting, and trying again. Mastery is never gained in the early stages of learning. We live in a world of filtered social media that only highlights rare or falsified perfection. The volume with which we are consuming this altered perception of life can be damaging to our resolve and demotivating. More and more people, especially young people, are afraid of trying anything new because they know they cannot do it perfectly the first time—and perfection is all they see reflected in the feeds of those they admire and would hope to impress.

Perfection cannot be the goal if you hope to accomplish anything of merit or impact. Experiences, learning, growth, and the joy of doing hard things need to be both the goal and the reward. It is through repetition that we learn, improve, and succeed.

This principle of improvement through repetition is illustrated perfectly by a story told by David Bayles and Ted Orland in their book, *Art & Fear*. On the first day of a photography class at the

University of Florida, professor Jerry Uelsmann divided the students into two groups. The first group was told that they would be graded based on the volume of photos they submitted over the course of the class. The second group was told that they would be graded on a single image to be turned in on the last day. At the end of the term, Professor Uelsmann was amazed to see that all of the top grades had come from the group that focused on quantity. It turns out that quantity of attempts reliably produces quality over time. Those focused on perfection never achieve it because they are paralyzed by the required "failures" of experimentation along the way, which are the essential elements when building up a mastery of a skill. You cannot skip this step.

Giving yourself permission to fail is a key element of being predictably successful.

CHAPTER 3 ROI SPRINT

Are you at a "rock bottom" of a professional challenge or embarrassment? Are there ways you can turn that struggle and the lessons you learned into your greatest asset? What opportunities lie for you on the horizon, upon which you can focus your attention and lift your sights beyond the challenges under your feet today? Are there opportunities for you to lead from behind and upset the status quo that would move you toward a strategic center for growth and development?

Recognize: What is your relationship with experimentation and failure? Do you limit yourself by avoiding tasks you know you cannot do perfectly today? How much of your time is spent in your comfort zone every day? Is it more than 80 percent?

Own: What new challenge can you give yourself to lower the percentage of time you're spending in your comfort zone and increase your chances of mastery and success in the long run?

Implement: Claim your power today and implement the changes that will bring you the most meaningful results.

CAREER ADVANCEMENT

There is a limit to what we can accomplish truly on our own. Betting on yourself in isolation can only carry you so far. We have to make a similar wager on the people with whom we work and the projects we choose. The only way you can create your unique mark on the world is to create a ripple effect that extends far beyond your own self and circle of direct influence. This requires you to champion and be championed by the people around you, creating an effect where you are all amplified together.

The most consistent way I have seen my and other's careers progress is when we are all moving toward a common goal. One of the tricks I learned early on is that the surest way to choose new projects that will advance your visibility and promotability is to identify key projects that simultaneously solve problems for your managers and that move them closer to accomplishing their most strategic objectives. If you can move something off your manager's task list and onto yours, which also allows you to learn a new skill and make strategic connections in the company, you have found the win-win formula that will get authorization every time.

Early on in my career at Amazon, I made an amateur mistake while trying to get my first salary increase. Through no effort on my part, I had been headhunted by Microsoft to work for a senior executive there. I wasn't actually interested in the job because I loved Amazon and working for Jeff, but I was tempted to interview because they were offering me significantly more money. I took Microsoft's offer to Jeff and said that I did not want to leave the company but asked if he would match the salary Microsoft was offering. To say that he was not pleased by my approach would be an understatement.

My mistake, I would later figure out, was that I made this exchange all about the numbers without making a case for why I was worthy of it. Not only did it appear disloyal to even consider other offers when what we were doing at Amazon was far more revolutionary at the time, but I had made a demand without offering anything in exchange. It wasn't backed up with a list of additional contributions I was going to start making.

From that point on, whenever I asked for a salary increase, I always started the conversation far in advance. I would tell my manager that I wanted to be considered for a promotion in six months, and I presented a specific, measurable list of milestone contributions I would make that would make me worthy of it and simultaneously advance the team's mission and my manager's key deliverables. That way, when the time came for the promotion decision to be made, we were both working off a common scorecard and toward a common goal.

Thankfully Jeff forgave my naive attempt at my first salary negotiation. I have never made that mistake again.

LEARNING BY DOING

In the early days of Amazon, most of us were tasked with doing things that literally no one had ever done before, so there had to be a high level of trust that we'd ask the right questions and be able to figure things out. All of this was at a time when the stakes couldn't be higher because of the scrutiny we were under from the board of directors, investors, and shareholders. We had to invent the future of e-commerce faster and better than any competitor just to remain in business.

It could have been tempting in this environment to opt out, assuming that my junior skills were inferior to the enormous challenges in front of us. But when I looked around, I saw impact coming from all levels of the company, so I asked myself, *Why shouldn't it come from me too?*

The right people put under the right pressure can create miracles of innovation that aren't replicable during times of comfort. Those who rose to the occasion in the early days of digital transformations are now the legends of the dot-com era. It was a time where there were only two extremes of results: innovation or irrelevance.

It was in this environment that Jeff heard an idea submitted by an employee, Greg Greeley, that eventually became Amazon Prime. Jeff realized that Super Saver Shipping, which was still in its infancy, could continue to serve those customers with more time than money, while Amazon Prime would serve those with more money than time. With this dual approach, the needs of virtually all customers could be met, entrenching a system of customer loyalty that would make Amazon the default retailer for customers' daily needs. It was something that had never been done before. This was the original subscription model of the digital era.

The idea for Prime came while the company was fighting competitors on multiple fronts. In 2004 Toys"R"Us sued Amazon, claiming that the company had violated an agreement about them being an exclusive seller of toys on the website. The holiday season had also been stressful, with frequent site outages and pressure from brick-and-mortar competitors, which were still growing at 17 percent a year. Amazon was worth $18 billion while eBay, which was a huge competitor at the time, was worth $33 billion. Amazon was up against giant competitors, and the path forward was unknown territory. It is amazing that, rather than bury his head in this problem, Jeff kept his eye on the long-term horizon and focused on what would make the company the most competitive and helpful to our customers.

The Amazon Prime concept was brainstormed by the senior leadership team on a Saturday morning at Jeff's boathouse and was announced during the annual earnings call just four weeks later. Our team averaged working between 110 and 120 hours per week during that month. We were in a fight for survival.

Rolling Up Your Sleeves

While the environment was stressful because of the sheer volume of things that needed to be done and invented from scratch, there was an undeniable, thrilling energy that swept us all up and carried us along. As a young employee in the CEO's office, I felt like the future of Amazon was in the front car of a roller coaster traveling at full speed while Jeff and our entire team frantically leaned out and built the track just ahead of us. This required a huge level of trust in each team member, no matter how senior or junior his or her role.

At that point in my early career, I didn't have the skills needed to own any major strategic initiatives, but I was smart enough to make myself available to assist the key players with anything they could possibly delegate to me so that nothing distracted them from delivering a miracle. This is how I learned how to run a "war room," as tech companies call the conference rooms housing the teams working around the clock on a time-sensitive launch, which was a vital skill in my future at Google. I learned to anticipate their needs and supply them before they could even ask for them.

I didn't care if my assignments in that room were glamorous. I was willing to roll up my sleeves and do anything. This often included intern-level tasks like midnight food orders, basic research assignments, or working with facilities to be sure the lights and heat weren't automatically shut off in the building at night or on the weekends. I didn't care! All that mattered to me was that I could be helpful and that this gave me my ticket into the room where the magic was happening. The experience of watching Jeff and his SVPs work in the war room has proven to be priceless countless times in my career since.

When Jeff first presented the idea of Prime to the board in 2005, they were skeptical. They rightly questioned how the company could offer unlimited 2-day delivery on over 1 million in-stock items (or as Jeff announced it "all-you-can-eat express shipping") for just $79 a year without bankrupting itself. If customers order a three-dollar toothbrush with free overnight shipping, the company could not make a profit. There had to be more to it.

Jeff was focused on decades-long growth, not current quarterly results. He favored actual revolutionary advancement and was not tempted by immediate shareholder satisfaction. He was playing the long game and, as he described it, digging a strategic moat around his customers. He was willing to sacrifice small results now for dominance later, but the investors were motivated by a different timeline, having lost almost everything in the recent dot-com bust.

The key initial factors in the Prime proposal were the cost of shipping and supply-chain optimization. During one critical board meeting, Jeff literally did the math for the board of directors, filling all of the whiteboards, with the Seattle skyline outlined behind him through the floor-to-ceiling windows on the fifteenth-floor conference room, and showed them exactly what price would need to be negotiated with shippers to make this loyalty plan work. Jeff Wilke, the SVP of operations, focused on the supply-chain system so that they could avoid as much air travel as possible for order fulfillment because sending a package by air was ten times more expensive than ground delivery. The board gave Jeff a short leash to make it all work.

With this limited green light, Jeff proceeded to negotiate a deal that no one imagined possible. His first efforts were thwarted by FedEx: they thought his terms were crazy and were confident that no other shipping partner would accept them. Jeff then took the bold step of diverting all Amazon-order traffic from FedEx to another shipping partner, at great short-term expense to the company, to prove to them just how much business they would lose if they did not negotiate the terms he wanted. It was a gutsy move! If they had called his bluff, Amazon likely wouldn't have survived. Jeff knew that the strongest card we had to play was tying our fates together.

His bet paid off. He got the terms he needed for the Prime program to be sustainable and profitable. Almost immediately after launch we saw that Prime members were spending more hours on the Amazon site and spending more money than any other customers. Amazon's long-term customer loyalty was born.

The fulfillment center protocols reduced inefficiencies in the ordering process and increased shipping speed while reducing the total shipping costs. The software developed by the team to coordinate the order fulfillments was revolutionary, producing dramatic results. No competitor was able to fulfill orders as efficiently as this proprietary software did. This breakthrough allowed Amazon to then launch and patent 1-Click shipping, with immediate and highly accurate delivery estimates for users.

Today we take these smooth systems for granted, but nothing had ever come close to this customer experience before. This innovative breakthrough came at the last strike of the countdown clock. This history-making project was only possible because Jeff fully trusted in the team and in the project vision, and the team fully trusted him as a leader. Every level of the company was needed in order to make this dream come to life—not just those at the top.

Endless Innovation Cycles

In my early years at Google, working for Marissa Mayer on the Product team involved a similar constant cycle of project launches and war rooms within the marathon of creating what Google is today. She consistently needed to have her team focus, pivot, and put in heroic efforts. It was both a stressful and a thrilling time for us all. Our entire team was very young, so we were all just making things up as best we could, trying to launch bigger, better, and faster than our competitors. At this point Google wasn't yet the default search engine for the world that it is today.

One of these memorable, endless, back-to-back product-launch cycles happened in 2008, when we had several major products launch just months apart that all required herculean efforts from our entire Product team. I focused a lot of my time on the teams tasked with launching the designer iGoogle home page feature and the transit application within Google Maps simultaneously. At first it was tricky to have so many sprint projects and war rooms happening at the same time, but this soon became a norm.

I used my war-room experience from my earlier Amazon days to set up a dashboard of launch milestones and to keep all of the action items prioritized and consistently on track so that Marissa and our entire team could use their time, energy, and resources as effectively as possible. I became the connector between the legal, engineering, UX/UI design, communications, and partnership teams, which were all collaborating to build something that was new to us all. This became the catalyst effect we all needed to get through the marathon-length list of deliverables at a sprint pace. It was exhausting and thrilling all at the same time.

iGoogle was a personalized version of the Google home page, where users could add gizmos in order to see their most commonly used apps at a glance all in one place and then select various products. For example, your personalized Google home page could have a preview of your Gmail, chats, news, and more, so that coming to the home page was a one-stop shop for everything you use every day. Remember that this was before smartphones provided this consolidation of information through apps in your pocket.

iGoogle was launched in 2005, but it didn't gain real traction for about three years. In April 2008, during this critical window of opportunity, we launched designer home page backgrounds with seventy artists, including Diane von Furstenberg, Tory Burch,

Marc Ecko, Jeff Koons, Oscar de la Renta, and even Coldplay, in an effort to make this home page space personalized and more beautiful. The idea was to drive user loyalty and to help motivate users to make Google their default home page—which was not a given at the time. Yahoo! had just recently lost their exclusive content deal with MSN, which gave us at Google a rare opportunity to recruit new users before Microsoft launched Bing the following year. These product launches were core to the company's future, and we knew that we might never have that chance again. We had to get this right, and we had to do it fast.

Marissa has an amazing eye for design, and this was reflected both in her stewardship of the clean Google home page but also in her personal style. She had close relationships with major fashion designers, and this opened doors for these unprecedented partnerships. I dedicated a lot of time and energy into crafting and orchestrating this unprecedented collaboration of engineers, designers, product developers, and others from all across the company. I had to become the central hub between the otherwise-decentralized teams that were essential for the launch's success.

The entire team was working an average of fifteen hours a day just to get everything done. I lived in Berkeley at the time and would take the first Google shuttle in the morning at 7:00 a.m. and the last shuttle home at 9:30 p.m. This was an hour-and-a-half commute each way in addition to my hours in the office. It was not unusual for me to miss the last shuttle of the day and need to borrow one of the Google fleet cars (which were available for employee use during the day for doctor's appointments and other errands if you had taken the shuttle in). We also often were in the office, or at a minimum on our laptops from home, all day on Saturdays just to keep our heads above water.

It was during this time that the city of Mountain View cracked down on Google headquarters about the number of employees who were literally sleeping and living full-time in the office because they saw no need to pay the steep rent prices for an apartment they never used. We had showers in the gym and laundry facilities in every building, which, when combined with the free food on campus, removed any need to ever go home. We had to literally make a rule that employees couldn't sleep at the office. I had to remove the big red sofa we had in the corner of our office for one-on-one conversations into the hallway just to be sure our team was compliant. Even then, people still slept on it occasionally.

Just a few months later, in April 2008, the iGoogle partnership launch was held outdoors in the Meatpacking District of Manhattan, just a few blocks from the Google New York office. I remember sitting in the front row under the night sky holding the final draft of Marissa's speech notes just before the launch event started and pinching myself because I was literally sitting between Tory Burch and Diane von Furstenberg, two self-made businesswomen whom I admire greatly. The surrounding old brick buildings in the Meatpacking District were glowing with LED-projected facades of the designers' iGoogle signature looks, and the juxtaposition of old and new American industry was thrilling and unforgettable.

The press coverage was very favorable, and the day felt like a huge success and an enormous relief. Our celebrations that night under the stars in New York felt like we had won the nerd version of the World Series.

What was not on our minds that night was that Apple had a similar idea for driving user interaction and would launch the original App Store in July of that same year, just a few short months after the iGoogle launch; with five hundred applications available, it would shift consumer behavior in a new direction. We launched the Android Market, the predecessor to the current Google Play store, one month after Apple's launch, in October, which would pivot all of our team's user-interaction focus away from iGoogle.

We were similarly unaware that the social network movement was about to hit the internet and derail the last-remaining relevance of iGoogle. But that was a pivot and a sprint saved for another day. This is the thrilling and maddening part of working in tech: the need for constant innovation never stops. You have to keep designing and being willing to kill off a product you put your entire heart into yesterday in order to build for tomorrow.

Just a few months after the iGoogle launch, in September 2008, we were back in New York to launch the transit feature in Google Maps with an event in Grand Central Terminal with our founders, Larry Page and Sergey Brin, at the microphones. Nowadays we all take for granted that you can arrive in almost any country in the world and navigate real-time walking, biking, transit, or driving directions from your mobile phone through Google Maps. At the time this was almost unimaginable to anyone except Google's founders.

The steps leading up to this launch event were long and took enormous vision. It was less than two years after we launched Google Street View, which required collecting photographs of every street on earth. Even internally at Google, it seemed like an impossible task and was met with some skepticism. Not only would we need to drive every street on earth with specially designed cars outfitted with proprietary cameras mounted on top and GPS trackers, but we would need to revisit each of those streets regularly to document updates.

There were governments to collaborate with and privacy concerns to consider and the need for enormous manpower and data processing, but this did not deter Larry or Sergey for a moment. The opportunity to serve our users with this additional ability to explore their neighborhoods or sites from faraway lands that they might never experience otherwise was too important to be swayed by the fact that it would take a lot of continual work to accomplish it. Eventually this would extend to mostly unattainable heights, like Kilimanjaro and the International Space Station.

While the launch event for Google Transit Maps itself was an enormous and unprecedented one that took nearly six months to plan and get permission for, it was a cakewalk in terms of complexity compared to the rest of what the company had gone through to create and deliver this revolutionary product.

I remember waiting for Sergey to arrive outside of Grand Central Terminal so I could walk him over to where the press event was taking place inside. I was watching for a car to pull up and drop him off, but instead Sergey arrived alone rolling up on his rollerblades with a huge smile on his face. It wasn't until we were inside and looked at the stairs up to the stage that we both realized that he hadn't brought any shoes to change into when he took off his rollerblades to make the speech. We debated for a moment whether he should just wear the rollerblades or make the speech in his socks. He settled on just wearing socks, and no one seemed to really notice.

Establishing a Sustainable Pace

My first desk at Google was about fifteen feet away from Larry and Sergey's shared office and a three-minute walk to the CEO's office in the building next door, connected by a skywalk. My conversations, late-night strategy chats, and code reviews with these inspiring executives became the internal narrative in my head that has driven my project management instincts across my career at Google and into my executive consulting after. It could have been easy to miss this learning opportunity by burying my head in my endless to-do list rather than getting up and asking questions. However, sometimes it's how we use the otherwise boring days or "easy" tasks that makes or breaks our careers far more than war rooms and emergency situations.

Around this same time in my career, I learned a counterintuitive lesson about stretch goals pacing while training for the Nike Women's Half Marathon in San Francisco. I am not a good or natural runner by any stretch. In fact, I had signed up for my first half marathon in 2012 before I had ever even run a 5K. This moment of seeming insanity started when I received a work email from a colleague one evening with a link to a donation page in his auto signature where he was raising money for leukemia research by running a half marathon. I clicked on the link and made a donation. Then I signed up for the race on the spot and decided to help raise money too. I am not an impulsive person so this was very out of character for me.

Undeterred by my inexperience, and lifelong hatred for running, I created a training schedule for myself in the nerdiest way possible by simply googling "how to train for a half marathon," printing out the training plan, and then getting to work. That first half marathon was in San Diego on a nice flat course. Training had been really hard and required a lot of sacrifices, but I had enjoyed the sense of accomplishment and empowerment outside of work. The next day, I signed up for the race in San Francisco six months later.

The Nike Women's Half Marathon is in a particularly hilly part of the city so I knew that I would have to do a lot of hill training to be ready. All of the hill training drills I read about online recommend that you do a series of hill sprints where you run up the hill and then catch your breath while walking back down to the starting point before beginning again. This turned out to be both highly effective and a disastrous approach. While this training did build up my hamstring muscles to power me up the many long hills on race day, it had failed to develop the quadriceps muscles on the front of my legs, which needed to be strong enough to handle the pounding of the downhill stretches that followed. The "easy" part of that race fatigued my unprepared quads so much that I couldn't walk down even a slight incline for almost a week after the race. I would have to turn around and walk backward!

In my career I've had moments of being blindsided by not performing well on seemingly easy tasks right in front of me because I didn't focus on training up those skills or strengths immediately in front of me, which I dismissed as easy and boring. If we focus only on the uphill battles, we won't be balanced enough to be a consistent team player. Similarly, if we train only within our comfort zones and specialize in the downhill efforts, we won't be ready for those critical uphill battles that inevitably come.

CLEAR FEEDBACK LOOPS

When I first joined Google, I was asked to write a list of goals for myself, upon which I would be evaluated at the end of my first quarter at the company. Google uses a system called OKRs, which stands for Objectives and Key Results. I had some limited experience with this system from when I was at Amazon because John Doerr was a board member at both Amazon and Google and had introduced this method to the founders. He has since written a fantastic book about this goal-alignment-and-fulfillment strategy called *Measure What Matters*.

OKRs are set on a quarterly time frame and cover a range of moonshot-level deliverables. When done correctly, OKRs allow for the leadership to set the direction of the company by establishing three to five key areas of growth for the company, and then the individual contributors and managers set their own audacious goals and deliverables within that framework. This system allows each employee, no matter how junior or senior, to feel that his or her contributions are directly tied to the company success and to feel empowered to have a major effect on that result.

At the end of my first quarter at Google, I felt pretty proud of what I had accomplished. I had gone from knowing absolutely nothing and no one in the company to being the hub of our team. I felt like I had done the impossible, and the OKRs I had written for myself were all solidly accomplished. And that, it turned out, was exactly the problem.

Imagine my shock when, instead of a glowing report card, my manager, Marissa, reacted with disappointment. She explained to me that I had been focused on tasks rather than actual key results. In effect, my "perfect performance" grade proved to her that I hadn't aimed high enough or challenged myself in meaningful ways. She was not interested in perfection. She wanted me to take the audacious goals of the company and stretch myself to deliver key results toward those goals within my own role.

Despite my experience with this goal-setting system while at Amazon, the first quarter's OKRs I wrote for myself at Google were not aimed at this higher impact. I had felt so overwhelmed by joining the team without any training or crossover with my predecessor that I got stuck in just delivering daily tasks rather than attempting any actual leaps forward, which is what the company needed from me most at that growth stage.

My first-quarter OKRs were all about tasks and systems. I wrote goals like "create a system for streamlining media and speaking requests and clearing out the backlog." While this summarized an important task that needed attention, it was not very ambitious. I had missed the entire concept of raising my sights from daily tasks to what we were trying to build as a company and my possible role in it.

Marissa's disappointed feedback in my goal-setting performance was a mental pivot point in my career. She gave me clear permission to set goals beyond my current abilities and to fail occasionally. It was so freeing to think that I would be rewarded if I aimed for something far outside my comfort zone and was able to deliver only 50 percent or 80 percent of what I had set out to do rather than delivering a consistent ten-out-of-ten score on tasks that were firmly in my area of expertise but that didn't move us closer to our audacious company mission and goals.

I realized that when I was focused just on tasks, I was solving the problems already under our feet. What I needed to do instead was take a future-looking-back approach and imagine the needs of Google and our users many years in the future and start solving for those needs before the moment arrived. For example, this changed the amount of energy I spent on the mechanics side of strategy off-sites. Rather than focusing solely on creating the perfect blueprints for operational systems, I realized I needed to focus my energy thinking about Google's mission and my role in delivering it.

This is a process commonly referred to as North Star alignment. I knew that Google's mission was to organize the world's information and make it universally accessible and useful. Our job on the Product team was to create the tools to deliver that mission into the hands of our global users. Marissa was tasked with finding these new ideas, designing the systems, producing cutting-edge code, and launching it in an accessible way. It finally clicked that the way in which I could have the most impact was to make Marissa's deliverables directly tied to mine.

My second-quarter's OKRs were much more ambitious and aligned with this unifying North Star. I set my ambition to "become the central resource on the Product team in order to streamline the brainstorming, designing, coding, and launching of core products" that quarter. That was a pretty audacious goal coming from me, the most junior person on the Product team. However, when Marissa signed off on this goal, I considered that to be both the permission and authority I needed to do anything necessary to accomplish it. For example, this gave me mental permission to get up from my desk and my never-ending task list and take a seat in the rooms where these things were happening, so that I could observe the current system, make recommendations, and take action to make them more efficient, streamlined, and connected. And it worked!

This was a subtle mental shift, but the results were dramatic. Not only did I meet my personal goal of learning and understanding how to run code reviews, where breakdowns happen between UX/UI designers and engineers, and the complexities of launch events from the communications and policy side; I also became a critical resource for my team. I had to tolerate stumbling through meetings I didn't understand at first and ask a lot of "dumb" questions that revealed my ignorance of the process, but this accelerated my learning and ability to contribute substantially. This tied my career growth to the team's success and created a virtuous loop, where my learning and visibility dramatically increased in sync. And visibility almost always leads to promotability.

Marissa consistently rewarded risk-taking and fought hard for our team's compensation and advancement accordingly. It was liberating to no longer need to feel shackled by expectations of perfection in order to feel valuable to my team and the company. Marissa taught me to consistently do things before I felt ready and to value learning rather than a "perfect" performance.

Proactively Seek Feedback

The OKRs process prompted me to not wait for formal quarter-end evaluations and to seek out consistent, honest, challenging feedback on a regular basis from as many sources as possible. When my teammates saw that I was asking for this feedback, they started freely sharing their observations about strengths I didn't yet see in myself, and they identified weaknesses that needed tending.

Through this approach, early in my time at Google, I effectively learned how to put myself in the driver's seat of my career and decide for myself what I wanted to learn and accomplish. For example, I remember offering to help the communications team during the second quarter of 2008 while they were overwhelmed with the volume and pace of our upcoming launch calendar.

In September, we launched the Google Chrome browser, which was an enormous amount of work for the entire company. And this major effort happened only two weeks before we launched the very first Android mobile phone. For the Chrome browser launch, we put together a forty-page comic explaining how Chrome worked to make it feel exciting and accessible rather than confusing our users. For the launch of the Android HTC Dream phone with T-Mobile, we focused on educating consumers about the advantages of open-source software, best-in-class notifications, and deep Google-product integration.

I had no idea what I was doing, and I absolutely learned more than I contributed to the team during that process, but the lessons paid dividends. Without volunteering to help with tasks that were far beyond my current expertise, I never would have learned to run major launch events, educate the public about emerging technologies, or coordinate massive internal collaborations. I had to ask a lot of questions, work longer hours to make up for my lack of experience and knowledge, and be willing to show my naivete to very senior members of our Product team.

Actively Create Your Future Self

I didn't realize at the time, or for many years to come, how rare it is for people to try and reinvent themselves through stretch goals throughout their career. I think the greatest gift living in Silicon Valley gave me was the concept that nothing is unchangeable or fixed—including myself. I later took this experience into my role while working for Eric Schmidt in the CEO's office and running major collaborative projects with much more intimidating emerging technologies, such as artificial intelligence. I could not have done that without being willing to take a seat at tables for those far senior to my job title and put in the hard work while exposing everyone to the ups and downs of my learning process.

I learned to be able to envision my "future self," as UCLA psychologist Hal Hershfield refers to it, as something within my control. Without being able to envision this new, evolving self, it would be impossible to be deliberate and purposeful about my risk-taking, growth, and learning in a meaningful way, and I would have missed out on promotions, projects, and advancements that have driven my career forward.

Why would anyone put herself through the hard work and occasional humiliation without the possible reward of this self-designed future identity? Most of us have identities wrapped up in the experiences of our past. But the good news is that, with some purposeful choices, you can change and shape your identity, the way you and others think about you, to be anything you want it to be, by taking on small, incremental challenges.

This process ended up giving me the amazing advantage of being able to grow my skills in a way that qualified me to work for Eric Schmidt, where this pattern continued. I took on projects that most people at my job level never would have experienced. I just needed to be brave enough to let my growth goals be known by Eric and other leaders in power and to show them how my accomplishment of these goals would benefit them as well. That created a natural executive-sponsorship relationship. It is also the path for official promotion.

Create a Promotion Plan

I have never once in my career had a manager who came to me and said, "Ann, I've noticed this untapped talent of yours and I was thinking about ways in which you could apply it and grow your influence." That just isn't going to happen. That kind of effort has to come from you. And I can tell you that when I became a manager myself, I was always thrilled to understand the growth goals of my direct reports and ways in which I could support them. It made my job so much easier as their leader and gave us all a united purpose.

When I wanted an advancement at work, I would go to my executive six months to a year in advance and lay out my plan. For example, when I wanted to become Eric's chief of staff officially, a job title that didn't yet exist at the company, I came to him with a self-evaluation of the tasks I already did that were at that level as well as a list of suggested skills I needed to develop with specific projects I wanted to take on that would give me the chance to learn them. Once we were in agreement and aligned with my growth, I then had a road map to promotion that focused on advancing both of our positions. Then I got to work.

I knew that if I was going to truly be a chief of staff, I needed to hold meetings with Eric's executives in his absence and have the opportunity and authority to make some decisions on his behalf. As a first step, I proposed a plan where I would meet with the leads of the communications and policy teams once a week to review all of the global needs and concerns and to formulate recommendations for how to address them. I would then take this detailed understanding of the company's needs and create a prioritized strategy proposal for how to address them. This was both an intimidating and thrilling learning curve, but it immediately increased our ability to take action and create the best outcomes for the company and our users. Some of my most valuable professional skills and deepest friendships have come from making these bold moves.

In my post-Google life, almost all of my CEO consulting clients have come to me with frustrations around the promotion expectations of some employees. Most of my clients are in the scale-up phase of growing, where they have specific budget runways and limited promotions because the company is lean and tenure simply cannot be correlated to automatic title or salary increases. I have seen both effective and detrimental approaches by their employees.

At the AgTech company, I saw a brilliant approach by a talented young employee, Emy, who saw a need at the company during a period of huge transition and took on a major project responsibility outside her core role simply because it needed to be done and no one else had the bandwidth or the cross collaborative relationships needed to take it on. She made her growth goals known to her manager and simply went to work at the critical moment in the company's history when they weren't sure they were going to survive. She made her team not only more effective but also more profitable. After months of heroic efforts, she was effectively given a golden ticket to take on any project she wanted in the company because she had proven herself to be invaluable.

Alternatively, I have seen countless examples of my clients' employees demanding raises or titles without considering how their contributions tie into the company's bottom line or an actual need for more senior roles. They just come in with an expectation of automatic advancement without taking responsibility for what they are contributing or what the company needs at that moment. I saw one employee who had been originally targeted for a critical new role at her company ruin her chances because she immediately asked for a disproportionate salary increase without proving her value or abilities or tying the request to specific performance targets.

Big companies have the advantage of having a more streamlined process for promotions, but the steps are often very small and slow. In start-ups you have the freedom to take huge career leaps forward because the growth of the company is often more rapid, but you will likely need to wait years before you're rewarded financially. I have seen countless start-up employees who need to think more like owners when charting out how they can become indispensable to their company and recognized as such. Both sides need to have honest conversations early and often to find this common ground.

It may or may not surprise you to hear that I never once got a formal, written performance evaluation from my CEO managers. I supplemented this lack of formal guidance by seeking out small, consistent moments and asking the hard questions in order to get real feedback about ways in which I could improve.

Performance reviews should be direct, specific, and actionable. Unfortunately, receiving this kind of feedback is a challenge for most workers, especially those who are high performers, because delivering this is a challenge for most managers. This is especially true for women, who often only receive feedback about their behaviors, rather than their skills. This leaves the burden on the individual to seek out feedback from managers and peers.

When I received vague feedback on my performance, it was up to me to break it down into guiding principles. If I received a general "good job," it was up to me to ask for specifics so that I knew exactly the elements to repeat next time. When my performance was subpar, I would have to force the conversation to get specific about an action plan for doing better next time. I would proactively come up with a plan for how to avoid this situation from happening again and propose changes I would make for better results. That way I had a specific action plan that was agreed upon and that I could implement with full confidence. I would then specifically ask for resources, training, and mentors to guide my next steps. This feedback never came unsolicited.

I had a friend in college who was incredibly smart. He made the habit of attending office hours with each professor at the start of a new course to tell him or her that he expected to receive a perfect grade in the class and would put in any work necessary to accomplish that goal. The professors were always shocked at this bold expectation, but he kept showing up every single week to discuss ways he could improve and put in the time needed to do so. This changed the way his professors interacted and thought about him.

This set a common expectation for both himself and the professors and eliminated any possibility of differing expectations of what success looked like and how it would be scored. He graduated college with a perfect grade point average and earned every single A. Most importantly, all of his professors knew his name and his talents in detail and thought of him when research projects and other opportunities came up that he wouldn't have known about otherwise. And when he started applying for graduate school, it was easy and natural for them to champion him with detailed letters of recommendation.

This method applies to professional environments as well.

CREATING MEANING IN WORK

Even beyond formal promotions, bonuses, or salary increases, what has been most important to me in my work has been maintaining a passion alignment. This takes more creativity and proactive action early in your career than in the later stages because, early on, there is often the largest delta between the jobs you're qualified for and those you hope to have, but at either end of the spectrum there are steps we can take to put ourselves in the driver's seat of our career and move ourselves toward joy and fulfillment in our work.

While I have primarily worked in supportive, innovative environments, I have seen that not every company or manager has the humility, experience, or training to be encouraging or even tolerant of employees wanting to expand their influence beyond their basic job description. Some prefer to keep those below them down out of fear that they will supersede them. Even if you find yourself in a situation like this, there are steps you can take to create meaning, growth, and expanded influence for yourself. This is possible even in very traditional work environments or in roles that are normally considered entry-level or "unskilled."

Amy Wrzesniewski is a professor at Yale who researches how people make meaning of their work in difficult contexts simply by reframing their work mentally. She has analyzed and documented the way in which some workers redesign the specific work that they do to better match their personal strengths and values so that they can amplify the sense of meaning they get from their jobs. Time and time again, we see that seemingly small actions can have a big impact on our happiness and effectiveness.

The differentiator, more than the actual job description, comes down to how we think about and experience our work. Professor Wrzesniewski categorizes these three mentalities as seeing our work either as a job (just a means to make a living), a career (a way to gain advancement and prestige), or a calling (a source of personal fulfillment and a way to do something valuable). This might appear to be a luxury only available to elite positions, but her research has proven that assumption to be false.

In her research, Professor Wrzesniewski studied hospital janitorial staff and asked them to categorize their work as either "skilled" or "unskilled." Those who felt a direct connection between their responsibilities and the healing process of the people in the hospital rooms that they were cleaning categorized their work as skilled labor. Fascinatingly, they had the exact same job description and assigned tasks as those who considered their work unskilled and therefore insignificant and less meaningful; in other words, "just a job." The difference between these mindsets correlated directly to not only their effectiveness in their work but in their satisfaction and joy in doing it. Our attitudes are everything as we set out to elevate ourselves beyond just a job or a career but into fulfilling a calling.

Resilience and thriving in our work, especially if we aren't in our dream jobs, is essentially a skill of mindset and perspective. There is a well-known story of three bricklayers who were tasked with reconstructing St. Paul's Cathedral in London after its destruction in the fire of 1666. The work was being led by Christopher Wren, the famous architect, who noticed extremely different outputs by three of his bricklayers. The first was progressing very slowly and carefully. When this worker was asked what he was doing, he said that he was working hard laying bricks to feed his family. This first worker saw his work as simply a job. The second worker was a bit faster, and, when asked what he was doing, he responded that he was a builder and was building a wall. He viewed his work as a career. The third worker, who was the fastest and most skilled, when asked what he was doing, responded that he was building a cathedral to the Almighty. This third worker saw his time laying bricks as a calling. All three workers had the same tools, their bricks were all equally heavy, and their tasks were equally taxing, but their perspectives on the purpose of their work shaped their output, performance, and, perhaps most importantly, their pride in their work.

Choose to build a cathedral in whatever work you do!

Creating a Road Map

No matter the starting point where we find ourselves, there are things within our control to move us closer to our ideals of mission and purpose in our work. Looking back on my career now, I can see that when I was proactively moving toward my "calling," I was the happiest in my work even long before I felt I had arrived in that zone.

I have taken this approach several times across my career. Whenever I felt stagnant or unchallenged in my role, I created a spreadsheet for myself to help take an analytical approach to my soul-searching for meaningful contributions I could make. In column A, I listed every single professional responsibility I currently had, from the mundane to the exceptional. Then, in column B, I carried over only the responsibilities and projects that made me leap out of bed with excitement in the morning. In column C, I took each of those things that excited me in column B and then wrote down what they would look like if supersized in a role I could imagine having in the next year or two. From these discoveries, I made my personal promotion plan based on the qualities, responsibilities, and projects that I wanted to have that would move me systematically closer to my goals. Some of those findings surprised me, others terrified me, and some felt like I should have been doing them long ago. The next step was to find a way to get myself from my current role to that job description and higher calling.

Armed with this analysis, I had a road map that outlined the steps that lay between me and my dream work. This seemingly small mental process has led me to more advancement and joy in my work than I ever dreamed possible.

I have been the most frustrated in my work when the percentage of my time spent on tasks that felt like my "job" was far greater than the percentage of time spent on tasks that felt like my "calling." I have had the most joy in my work when I took the brave steps to insert more meaning into it. Professor Wrzesniewski suggests that we start this process by identifying what our motives, strengths, and passions are and then creating a list of tasks we could take on in our current role to shift the balance toward those while still performing our core job deliverables for which we were hired.

Recognizing Opportunities

One of my main tasks during my early years at Google was to collaborate with Google's famous APMs, or associate product managers; my manager, Marissa, created and ran the APM program. The company, even in the early years, didn't have any lack of talented applicants. However, Google has such a unique working environment that they recognized early that they needed an accelerator program to advance internally grown leaders who were not only the best engineers in the world but who also understood how to actually get things done at Google.

The APM program was created originally as a bet between Marissa and her manager, Jonathan Rosenberg. Google grew so fast in those early years that it became almost impossible for new employees to navigate this system and be productive. Marissa was one of the very few people in the company who knew how to navigate this increasingly complex system of small teams and relentless launch cycles. Everyone else had a siloed view. The need for more help was immediate. Marissa bet Jonathan that she could hire smart people right out of school and train them up to be impactful product managers faster than he could hire outsiders who are more experienced and senior. Her bet paid off.

Each year a small, elite class of about twenty APMs come into Google for a two-year rotation in the program. They are partnered with more experienced managers and are thrown into the most valuable projects the company is working on right from day one. Equally important, they were forced to rotate across several teams for a deeper understanding of the company and tech before "graduating" two years later and moving on to run major divisions of the company. The APM program provided the network that these talented young engineers needed to be successful.

For almost all of the APMs, Google was their very first job. They were young and smart and direct from the best universities in the world. I decided I needed to implant myself firmly in this group and benefit from the program that I had been tasked to help run. I loved partnering with my friend and office-mate Diana, who managed the program.

Each year the graduating class of APMs took a round-the-world trip to visit our most strategic growth markets and understand the particular needs of those users to inform their future product-development work. Many of the graduates of this program have gone on to run major product divisions for Google. My early years at Google were spent with amazing APM graduates like Brian Rakowski, who Marissa tasked in his first year to run all of Gmail and is now the VP of product management, and

Bret Taylor, who cofounded Google Maps. Other graduates have gone on to found major companies of their own. I saw this as a repeated opportunity to create my own growth role and assume this training for myself while simultaneously helping to lead it.

While traveling with the latest class of APMs in 2007 to Japan, China, India, and Israel, I received an unexpected invitation. Shimon Peres's office emailed me to see if Marissa Mayer would be available to meet with Peres while we were in Tel Aviv. Peres was newly elected as the ninth president of Israel, and he took very seriously his role as president to link the founding generation of Israel with the future generations. He saw technology and innovation as an essential role in the long-term viability of his country and people.

I was immediately excited about this invitation because I realized it was the perfect opportunity: my personal goals to increase my influence through global politics and technology overlapped with my team's mission to better serve our global users and the company's mission to make information universally accessible. This was a chance to move myself into that zone of fulfilling my calling rather than just doing a job.

I happily worked all night with our local policy team to put together a briefing document, anticipating all of the topics and requests that might come from President Peres. This was my first time owning a briefing for a meeting with a head of state, so I was tireless and thorough in my preparation to the point of memorizing the entire document. Marissa knew that I had taken international studies in school and was passionate about the politics around international business relationships. I had been very open in sharing my interests, background, and larger career ambitions with her during our time working together, and now was the moment for that boldness to pay off. Marissa thoughtfully invited me to join her in her one-on-one meeting with Peres. As we prepared for the meeting in the car, I was both terrified and thrilled.

We arrived at the president's office more than an hour early, anticipating heavy security procedures. The security screening time gave me a chance to calm my nerves and savor the experience once it began. After all of the formality of security, we entered Peres's office wing, which was strikingly calm, warm, and relaxed by comparison. President Peres had been a long-serving prime minister of Israel and was the chosen protege of David Ben-Gurion, Israel's founding father, at the age of twenty-eight. There was something special about Shimon Peres that was obvious immediately upon meeting him.

He welcomed Marissa and me into his office, and the three of us talked for an hour alone there. He was a gifted speaker, not only on the world stage. Even when talking one-on-one, his seemingly fleeting observations were particularly insightful. He had a way of elevating your comments and ideas to a new level and of creating something unforgettable. Peres had won the Nobel Peace Prize twelve years earlier for his peace talks with the Palestinian leadership during his time as foreign minister under Prime Minister Rabin. While sitting in his office that day, it was easy to imagine how those skills had come into play in those tense negotiations a decade earlier.

President Peres talked to us about his continued work in his foundation, Peres Center for Peace and Innovation, which had the aim to "promote lasting peace and advancement in the Middle East by fostering tolerance, economic and technological development, cooperation, and well-being." There were many opportunities for collaboration given our initiatives at Google. I left that meeting knowing that it was a day I would never forget, and that something had changed in me.

I had worked all night to prepare Marissa for that meeting, memorized a briefing document, and had passion for the topic but my learning that day could have stopped there were it not for Marissa's incredible leadership and focus on growing the talents of her team. I now had confidence that Marissa was a leader who would embrace this kind of growth experience for all her employees—including me. A big part of Marissa's legacy and enormous impact at Google stemmed from her gift for identifying and hiring early talent into her team, empowering them through aspirational challenges, and fighting hard for their future opportunities. Marissa could have focused solely on her own impact and ambition, which were enormous, but she didn't.

Marissa had a master's from Stanford in artificial intelligence and was employee number twenty at Google, hired as the first female engineer. Rather than rest on her own talents, Marissa also built up a team of loyal, game-changing, talented employees who changed the direction of the entire company and increased her impact many times over through extended influence. The ripple effect of Marissa's hires is incalculable within tech, even beyond Google, as these entrepreneurs, trained personally by her, have gone on to lead and found countless tech companies. I have always felt a huge responsibility to honor her investment in me and make my own impact reflect well on her.

After this experience, I set my sights on spending as much time in my career as I could in performing my calling and to be a leader like Marissa, who created these opportunities for everyone around her where others might only see limitations.

CHAPTER 4 ROI SPRINT

Is there an opportunity in your company or team where you can roll up your sleeves and get access to a room you wouldn't have been invited into otherwise? Can you shift the balance of your work from a "job" to a "calling" by creating a road map to becoming your ideal "future self"? What promotion plan can you create to put yourself on the leadership track today?

Recognize: What is your company's and team's mission? How can you better align yourself with this North Star and move yourself into critical projects directly tied to that?

Own: What will you propose to your team or manager this week that will stretch your abilities while simultaneously easing their burden? How can you become more visible and mission-critical?

Implement: Get visible by setting up meetings with key stakeholders this week and explain your growth vision.

GETTING A SEAT
AT THE TABLE

I have spent most of my career in rooms with some of the most powerful people in the world. This fact has been both an enormous privilege and the greatest personal challenge of my life. Now, I'm not asking anyone to play a violin for me; I am overwhelmingly grateful. However, this fact means that at the beginning of my career, and honestly in countless moments since, I have spent a lot of time feeling intimidated, awkward, and out of place. The challenge of learning to realize my own worth as the junior-most and least-prestigious person in the room could easily have paralyzed me and inhibited my progression. Countless times it would have been easier to shrink into the corner or opt out.

Perhaps there are a few people in the world who have the ego and confidence necessary to accept privilege by default, but I think that most of us feel like we need to earn our place in the

room. Because I started my career in my early twenties working for some of the wealthiest and most powerful bosses in the
world, I was thrown into this room when I was at my most junior,
ugly-duckling stage of my professional growth. Unlike most
people who work their way to the top in the traditional step-by-
step way, I hadn't had a full career to prepare for it. Every single
day was thrilling and terrifying.

I realized early that I needed an action plan if I was going to
not only survive but thrive in this space. I needed to quickly learn
how to do three key things:

- Get over imposter syndrome
- Streamline systems
- Claim a place at an already full table

The pace of the early years in the technology companies I
joined meant that I would either quickly sink or learn to swim.
The trouble was that I felt like all the swimmers around me were
Michael Phelps and like I was still wearing my little arm floaties.
Given this discrepancy, I had to find a way to still add value, or I
needed to get out of the pool. And I didn't want to get out.

GET OVER IMPOSTER SYNDROME

Everyone I worked with at both Amazon and Google had elite
backgrounds and educations. I constantly felt like I was literally
the only person at these companies who didn't go to Stanford,
Harvard, or MIT. I had attended public schools and universities
my entire life. Even my PhD was at a state school, albeit a top-ten

university. It took me a full decade to realize that that could be a strength and not a weakness.

For an embarrassingly long time, I would insert early into every conversation with a new person the fact that I had been recruited to Google out of my PhD program. I found that to be the easiest and most consistent way to prove to them that I was smart in a single sentence. It was a knee-jerk reaction to constantly try and prove that I deserved to be there. I spent a long time feeling like I was not enough. Even in high school, before my crazy career started, I had a recurring dream that a school administrator would come into one of my Advanced Placement classes, loudly ask the teacher why I was there, and say that I didn't belong there and should be moved to a more basic-level class. This deep-seated fear of not being smart enough to belong among those I considered more naturally talented was a burden I unnecessarily carried for decades.

Building Your Squad

The most effective way I found to battle my natural imposter syndrome was to surround myself with the right people. Before I could ever be ready for an inspirational mentor, I needed a squad of people who were simply a step or two ahead of me in my journey. That has been my most consistent tool for being effective rather than intimidated. These people would be my right-hand guides.

Within my first week at Amazon, I found the essential members of my first squad. The most important member was my teammate John, who took me under his wing. He helped me not only by peer-reviewing my work before I presented anything to

Jeff but also by translating what my assignments even meant and giving them context within our larger company goals. It would have been a huge mistake if I had shied away from asking him questions and pretended to understand everything that was going on. I even had to ask him what common tech acronyms meant— such as SQL, CRO, B2C, TL;DR, SaaS, SEO, and others—that later became second nature to me.

Once I understood what the assignments given to me even meant, I then needed to build up a core relationship with partners around some of the niche skills at which I needed to become quickly proficient. This included the flight coordinator I worked with at the charter jet company we used during my first year at Amazon. I had never booked a private jet and had no idea how to do so. I learned quickly that it's nothing like booking a commercial flight. The first questions our flight coordinator asked me was if I preferred a Gulfstream or a Bombardier Learjet and which FBO I wanted to use at the destination. I literally had no idea what that question even meant. I also learned quickly that I needed to partner closely with our security team to learn to do risk evaluations for external meeting venues and even small but important details like never booking hotel rooms in a floor higher than the seventh because that is the highest a firetruck's ladder is able to extend for evacuations. And these were just the basics! The complexities of my job reached far higher, and my squad of advisors was essential for curing me of overwhelm and helping me focus on what actually brought impact.

Unfortunately, not every team I joined across my career was a good experience from the start. I have had my fair share of frustrating team environments. At one point in my career, I unknowingly joined a team with an uncooperative teammate. This teammate found my recruitment to be a personal slight to her and a threat to her status on the team. She was the most junior person on the team and desperately wanted to be acknowledged for her work and promoted. She saw my hiring, as someone several levels senior to her, as something that would block her promotability.

She made my life very difficult from day one in every way imaginable. She was not only rude and critical of me, but she occasionally went so far as to actively sabotage my work by changing or deleting documents I wrote in an effort to make me look bad in front of executives. Eventually, I came to dread each day even though I absolutely loved my job and the tasks I was being given. The slightest thing would set off her insecurities and would begin a day of aggressive competition with me.

Our executive was never aware of her behavior or the situation I was in. My manager actively worked to coach us through it, and we felt, at the time, like it didn't need to be escalated further than that. In retrospect, I think that was a mistake because others who interacted only with this difficult teammate came to judge our executive by her bad behavior, which wasn't a fair reflection, especially since this executive had been shielded and was unaware of the behavior at all.

I tried everything to help my teammate to feel more relaxed and collaborative. We hosted morning office hours together on video conferences for issues in our global team so that we could collaborate on something we both cared about. I talked to her for hours about her work and got to know her personally.

Despite some wonderful moments of calm and humor, this competitive behavior lasted for over two years. I came to feel so self-conscious that I thought I was overreacting or making it all up in my head. When she called me on the phone out of the blue, almost a decade later, to apologize and admit all the ways in which she sabotaged my work, I felt an enormous sense of relief that it had, in fact, been real and that I did not imagine it.

Through this experience, I established my personal value system, by which I have judged every professional opportunity since and which I have taught my consulting clients to adopt in their own companies. I decided that two factors were very important to me in my work life. First, I wanted to work directly for a leader whom I admired and wanted to become like. Sometimes this meant that I was okay with being given tasks that were themselves less fulfilling because it was worth the benefit of being exposed to the kind of leadership I wanted to learn to emulate. Second, I wanted to be personally challenged and constantly up-leveling my skills. Both of these things were true in my role with the toxic teammate, so I stayed despite the other challenges. I promised myself that if one or both of those things disappeared, then I would leave.

Similarly I had a consulting client at a scale-up company in the midwestern United States who had very ambitious career goals but who was constantly thwarted by her manager. She did all the right things: she put in the work, took on projects no one else wanted to do, set up a growth plan, and even started taking graduate school courses at night and on weekends to increase her skills. The frustrating thing was that the role she wanted was desperately needed at the company, but she was blatantly being overlooked and actively disrespected.

After a year of solid effort, she finally came to the realization that she would need to either change teams or leave the company in order to progress. It was a gut-wrenching decision because she felt so loyal and had put in so much work, but she left when she realized that her manager was not the type of leader she wanted to become and that she would not be able to grow there. Leaving that team was the right decision for her, even though it felt like a defeat at first.

Creating a Dream Team

Later in my career, when Eric transitioned from CEO to executive chairman three years after I joined his team, we both had to invent our roles from the ground up while all of his other direct reports were moved to other teams in the company. I took this as an opportunity to up-level to chief of staff in conjunction. While my responsibilities shifted dramatically and immediately, I had to fight hard for the formal title. It took me *years* to convince human resources to make it official. At the time, Google didn't have any formal chief-of-staff roles, and the title wasn't pervasive in Silicon Valley as it is now.

I was suddenly doing what felt like the work of ten people, and I was only successful because I was able to manage executives with whom I had strong relationships of trust and with whom I created new collaborations. I set the meeting agendas, made strategic recommendations, frequently represented the CEO in meetings, and reviewed and approved high-level project decisions on his behalf. Ready or not, I had stepped into his spotlight.

I could not sustain this pace or impact alone. I had to build up a new team from scratch and create a new business model for our office. I needed to build a dream team.

I wanted to bring people on board who had a diversity of experiences, backgrounds, talents, and interests. I didn't want to hire anyone that I wouldn't categorize as more talented than me. I needed the bar to be incredibly high to meet the goals Eric and I had set. I was unwilling to hire anyone who wasn't capable of replacing me tomorrow. This takes a lot of trust as a manager, but I knew that hiring this team would push me every day to improve my game, demand innovation, and increase my impact in substantial ways.

I learned this principle of hiring-up by watching how my CEO managers and clients build their teams. I realized that, at the CEO level, you are always managing people with skills that surpass your own in specific areas of expertise. Sometimes that meant that the lower-level executive went to a more prestigious school or had a more advanced degree than their executive manager. In order to become the best leader possible, you need to be able to manage people with top skills and not allow ego or competitiveness to creep in. High impact teams bring out the strengths and best in each member and demand extreme collaboration to bring those parts into a single team effort.

I ended up creating a team that was so effective, Eric would eventually tell me, eight years later, that it was "embarrassingly good" because it put to shame every other team around us. Designing the team model came easily. The key and most challenging part was finding and hiring the right people.

The first person I brought on board was Kim, who had worked for Google's cofounders, Larry and Sergey, in the very earliest years of Google. She had the core company knowledge and relationships I needed for her to hit the ground running. She was a godsend and helped me keep my head above water. Originally she came on as temporary help but she ended up staying permanently because the work was so rewarding and we had so much fun doing it together.

Kim and I worked day and night just to keep up with the daily demands. I knew that we couldn't sustain that sprint pace forever. It took me almost a year to convince Eric that we needed another member of our team.

Knowing that Eric was a data-driven guy, I eventually set up a spreadsheet: column A showed him all the basic, core responsibilities we were covering. In column B he could see the projects we were taking on that were above and beyond our baseline deliverables. And then I set his sights on column C, which included my vision for the impact we could have and projects we could take on if we brought on a highly skilled third member of the team.

That spreadsheet convinced Eric that it was worth the additional team member in order to get to my vision for the impact we could have with this team of experts. What I hadn't considered was that Eric's core hesitation actually was about not wanting to build up an "entourage." He had just reassigned every single direct report he had had as CEO except for me, and he wanted to run our team as lean as possible. Once I made the case for all the things we could accomplish with high-level talent, that hesitation was resolved, and I got the support I needed.

I spent six months searching for the right person to join our team. Eventually we found Brian, who was in a similar role working with a hedge fund CEO in London. I hired him sight unseen after only video interviews, and he took the risk and moved from London to California and joined our band of dreamers and doers. We made a big bet on each other, and it was one of the best decisions I've ever made professionally.

I designed our team of strong players to be interchangeable, like three bodies with one mind. While I was the manager of our team and ultimately responsible for our collective successes and failures, I wanted the team structure to be flat and for each person to feel an equal sense of ownership and opportunities for growth. We each had our own strengths that complemented the others' areas of weakness.

I knew I had no space on the team for competition among us, no space for any kind of progress-limiting hierarchy of status or project assignments. Our team metric was tied so that success was only possible if we were completely united. There was no vying for the "cool" projects, and no one had more visibility than anyone else. I never kept information from the team, and we never competed with one another. We each gladly stepped in to help one another at any time with any task and never kept score. I have never seen a team work so cohesively.

Naturally, I made mistakes along the way as I built up our team. I had never managed a full team before, nor had I been formally trained to do so, and I was trying to figure it all out on my own while under an enormous burden and massive volumes of work. While we were experimenting with this unconventional team model, we all had to make adjustments as things broke or failed as we experimented. There were times when my team members were frustrated with me. I failed many times and accidentally stepped on toes while trying to be sure nothing fell through the cracks and while doing quality control.

Seamless collaboration often comes down to the small, unglamorous details. I set up a team Google Doc to track all of our action items and a daily sync meeting that we never, ever skipped, not even if we were on different sides of the world or if we were sitting right next to one another all day. We had a shared team email address that we religiously copied on every single email we sent so that we would all be in the loop on every project at all times.

This team exceeded my expectations in every way. They pushed me to think creatively, to dream unapologetically, to stand tall when faced with failures, and to lead with compassion and joy through uncharted waters.

I learned that the best way to be an impactful manager is to hire people who push you to be your best and whole self every day. I showed up every day with my A game, even when I felt worn down, so as never to be the weak link on our team. With them at my sides, I could safely lift my head up and keep my vision on the long-term horizon; I could work to move Eric and the company strategically forward while knowing that everything would be managed perfectly today. This team became my family and my inspiration.

With a solid team in place, we were able to tackle enormous projects and do things no one at the company had ever done before. I thrived in this new focus, which was aligned with my personal interests, values, and growth goals. I seized the opportunity to learn and lead as much as possible. I was in vulnerable professional situations a lot because we were constantly doing new things every day and implementing things before we had perfected them. I learned to let go of the instinct to be perfect and instead focus on what we were contributing.

STREAMLINE SYSTEMS

One of the greatest advantages of working at an early stage tech company was that literally everyone was making things up as they went because they were constantly doing things that no one had ever done before. I tried to remember these lessons of grit, experimentation, and quick pivoting even years later in my career when I continued to make mistakes when taking on new challenges. This was absolutely true while I was learning to manage teams effectively.

I spent one summer managing several projects in the Google London and New York offices. This meant that I had to balance partnering with my European or East Coast colleagues during the day and manage my team at headquarters in California during the evenings. I learned the hard way how difficult it can be to lead a team remotely despite all of our shared docs, daily video conference syncs, and careful project planning. I wasn't available for impromptu sanity checks or friendly chats over coffee as I normally was. I also wasn't able to give the same detailed level of guidance and feedback that I had previously given when we sat side by side all day.

Before I left California, I had anticipated some challenges with the distance so I had set up a weekly one-on-one with each of my direct reports anticipating this need to connect individually, even though we were all meeting daily as a group for at least an hour on video. As time went on and nights got longer and longer for me in London, these one-on-ones became less frequent and I made the mistake of allowing them to become optional. That meant that we only came together when something was already broken rather than me being able to anticipate issues in advance and insert early solutions. This took a toll on my team and myself during that summer. Looking back now, I see the enormous value of having learned that lesson back in 2017 before the entire world was forced to work remotely in 2020.

Some of the most valuable lessons I've learned in collaboration, leadership, and management have come from collaborating with people outside my own team and still driving results.

Elevating Opportunities

Larry and Sergey, the cofounders of Google, famously did not want to have assistants or direct reports for almost a ten-year stretch. They wanted to remain free to follow ideas whenever they arrived, and they wanted to have the space they needed to invent the future of technology—which never happens during a formal meeting in a conference room. They had experimented with a support team in the early years of the company but ended up disbanding the team. They decided that they were better off without anyone attempting to own their time or force them to do things they didn't want to do. The catch was that sometimes the company really did need them to show up, and in those times I was occasionally called on to step in.

Larry and Sergey had become comfortable with me when I worked for Marissa, primarily because our offices were just a two-minute walk apart, down the same hallway. Once I was working directly for Eric, they started tapping me for occasional projects. While none of this was technically my job, I could think of no better way to serve the company and learn about leadership and strategy than to assist the founders with special projects.

The projects I did for the Google founders were somewhat unpredictable. Sometimes they would ping me to host special guests and give them a campus tour. One day they pinged me without notice to help them with a VIP guest, and I found myself walking around campus with the actress Natalie Portman for an hour and explaining our corporate culture before she made a surprise appearance at our weekly company town hall meeting, TGIF. She is one of the most impressive, gentle, and intelligent people I have ever met—in case you were wondering—and for me that is a very high bar.

These random projects could have easily felt like a distraction from my already-enormous job, but I knew it was a privileged opportunity to learn from and work closely with leaders whom I greatly admired. So I kept on saying yes.

One day, Larry came to me and said that he wanted to spend one afternoon a week informally meeting with the top engineers at Google. He missed the days when he could just walk up to a random engineer's desk and ask, "Whatcha working on?" The company was too big, with then over twenty thousand people, and he didn't want to lose touch with the employees or the core engineering issues. He asked me to help him fix that problem. For the next six months, I set up "Eng Chats" for him across the company.

To everyone's horror, Larry didn't want anything scheduled formally. He just wanted to "pop by" impromptu where he was needed most and learn about the most important projects of the day. I set up a spreadsheet with a list of proposed engineers for him to start meeting with, and I used it to track his progress and continually reprioritized and added suggested names. I met with Larry for three hours each Thursday to help make these conversations happen. I prepared mini prioritized lists each week based on what was most pressing at the company that day and printed maps of the campus with the engineers' locations so he could just wander by.

Larry appreciated this organized yet hands-off approach to orchestrating his drop-by Eng Chats. I used this unprecedented opportunity to get to know all of Google's top engineers and to build up a strong working relationship with them, as well as to build a full understanding of the company's core strategy and strengths. This habit of staying closely tied to developing technologies and prioritizing conversations with his most competitive engineering talent prepared Larry to take over as CEO of his own company after Eric's ten-year tenure.

Managing Up

There was a reason I was tapped for this particular project with Google's cofounder. I had built a reputation for doing my homework. The "homework" process is not glamorous, but it can be career changing. I had spent a lot of late and lonely nights reading, studying, listening, and making observations about what the company needed today and what it would need to be successful tomorrow. To do this effectively, I knew that I needed a vast amount of exposure to different situations and opinions in order to qualify myself for the rooms I wanted to sit in in the future, so I consistently sought out projects that would give me that perspective. I built a reputation, and the opportunities followed. This took years of concentrated efforts.

Even with all that preparation, I had to be very thoughtful in how I took on this project with Larry. There is an art to managing-up to someone very senior to you. Most importantly, you need to lay a groundwork of trust. You need to first prove your abilities, your loyalty, and your courage in small, daily tasks. Most of the time, this part feels invisible, and it may be. It's easy to lose sight of its value as other daily tasks pile up, but this is how you build a firm foundation of the work, collect the right data, and gain an understanding of the core company strategy and motivations of your executive and team.

I have seen people jump into wanting projects, promotions, and the spotlight without having done any foundation building, and they miss the mark. This can be extremely damaging to your reputation and the momentum of the entire team, so it's essential not to hurry past the phase of consistently putting in the hard work of learning and contributing.

This gives you an opportunity to identify things you can take off the plates of your senior leadership, which frees them up to maximize their output, focus on their most impactful work, and delegate tasks to you, which allows you to grow in skills and influence. This is the win-win we always want to focus on when managing up! When your superiors feel comfortable delegating to you, that is when you are able to step up onto a bigger stage that you wouldn't have had access to otherwise.

You need to be the one the management turns to when they need things to run smoothly.

One of my consulting clients had a period of rapid growth and all the usual problems that come with it. This CEO identified someone within the company who he felt could be a perfect right-hand partner to whom he could delegate. Unfortunately, once this person saw himself as the heir apparent, he stopped being effective and became his own worst enemy. He said all the right buzz words, but he didn't get the critical things done. He became really inconsistent in the standards of his work and lost the trust of his team. The promotion was his to lose, and eventually he did.

We had to hire externally to replace him and recover what had been lost. This new leader was one who leads by example by working alongside her team and who takes on any critical project, no matter how unglamorous, rather than being distracted by the spotlight of her title. By doing so, she freed up the CEO to focus on the core growth areas, which then led the company into a competitive advantage.

Be the Calm in the Storm

Hillary Clinton had just written her memoir *Hard Choices* and was going to be in Silicon Valley in three days as part of her book tour.

Her deputy chief of staff, Huma Abedin, reached out to me to see if Google would like to host a book talk between Hillary and Eric Schmidt. She called me on a Friday while we were kicking off our annual thought-leaders conference in another state, and they wanted to do the talk in Mountain View on Monday, the morning after we were set to return.

Eric agreed that it would be a great idea, and so I set to work coordinating and delegating the logistics that came with hosting, which were complicated not only because it would be a huge event on campus, but also because a former First Lady would be involved. I had to collaborate with multiple teams over the weekend, including Corporate Communications, Events, Legal, Google Security, and the Secret Service. The hard work paid off, and Eric and Hillary were onstage right on schedule on Monday with a huge crowd at headquarters and thousands more watching on YouTube.

Hillary offered to do a book signing after the event for Google employees, so her assistant arranged to have books delivered in advance. It became clear pretty quickly that they had not anticipated the high demand and that the books were going to run out before we got through the line of people waiting for their turn.

One of my event volunteers came rushing up to the table where I was standing next to Hillary and practically shouted, "We have a problem!" Clinton's assistant rushed that person away from the table and responded calmly, "We don't have problems. We have solutions." She swiftly solved the concern by promising that Clinton would sign books that night for anyone waiting in line who didn't receive one and that they would still be able to meet her now and take a photo. Solution delivered.

That moment has stayed with me all these years later because that is a simple illustration of my philosophy and my secret for success in my job as chief of staff. I never presented anything to

Eric without having first researched all of the issues thoroughly, gathered the essential data, and prepared several suggestions for actions to take. I never wanted to just present a problem; I wanted to arrive with solutions. This is the key to managing up.

CLAIMING YOUR PLACE AT AN ALREADY-FULL TABLE

At times it was intimidating for me, as an individual contributor, to be consistently surrounded with top CEOs who were also pushing every day to level-up their impact. I had to confront some consistent feelings of intimidation and not allow them to distract me from both the privilege and the corresponding task at hand. When you're leveling up, there will always be a feeling of fear or discomfort. You just have to remind yourself in those moments that that feeling is a sign that you're doing it right!

As I committed myself to increasing my contributions over time, I had to be creative in streamlining processes, delegating tasks, and bringing in new partners and practices to free up time to focus on strategic decision-making and content contributions. It took some time to get it right, and there were some awkward moments along the way as we all adjusted. I wanted to make a bigger impact within Google and beyond, and I saw ever-increasing opportunities to do so.

Bring Your Own Folding Chair

In the summer of 2014, my team was dealing with high-level political issues, which meant we spent most of our time in Europe for several months. One of these strategic areas of focus was a meeting with the newly crowned king of Spain, after the sudden abdication of his father, at the royal palace in Madrid. I had worked with our local policy team to write the briefing for the meeting between Eric and the king with the suggestions Google wanted to make for how to encourage and incentivize entrepreneurism in Spain, which was still reeling from the economic recession of 2008. Spain desperately needed to benefit from fresh policies under the new king's leadership.

We had had several high-level meetings in Madrid at the Google for Startups Campus and a colorful dinner with cultural leaders including artists, filmmakers, and musicians at the residence of the US ambassador to Spain, James Costos. I felt a bit awkward in the room while surrounded by famous Spanish influencers, but I knew I couldn't let that prevent me from doing my job effectively. The most memorable of all was the meeting at the king's palace in Madrid. This was where the awkwardness came to a peak for me.

The drive up to the palace was like out of a movie. We left the main street and drove up a narrow road lined with perfectly spaced trees and no other buildings in sight until we pulled up at a private entrance. When we arrived in the reception area, our Google policy lead was horrified when she saw that Eric planned to bring me into the room with the king, who himself was not staffed by anyone. Eric stood his ground, without any encouragement from me, and explained that it was important that I join him and that I wasn't going to be made to wait uselessly in the lobby.

I sat in that room silently, with my heart pounding in my ears, until I was called on specifically for my thoughts. I felt enormous pressure to prove Eric right—that my presence in the room was of value. Eric was famous for having a neutral person in the room on whom he could call for summary observations and proposed next steps. And this time it was no different. I do not think my contributions made any substantial difference in the course of that meeting with the king. However, it absolutely made a substantial difference in my confidence to bring my own chair to the table even if I'd been told that it was full. This was a light bulb moment!

But now I realized that I didn't just want to be in the room where important things were happening; I wanted to earn my own seat at the table.

What Makes You Different Makes You Worthy

I regularly experienced this up-leveling intimidation feeling when I partnered with Eric's venture capital firm, Innovation Endeavors, to put together an annual tour in Tel Aviv of world-renowned scientists, academics, and entrepreneurs. On our second trip in 2015, we met with the amazing minds at the Weizmann Institute to look for ways in which artificial intelligence could advance lifesaving medical technologies. I was far outside my areas of expertise, to say the least!

I remember one particular dinner hosted in the private residence attached to a prominent museum where I took countless pages of notes solely on the terms and references that I did not understand and wanted to look up later. It would have been easy to slip into moments of silent intimidation, and I actively had to fight these self-limiting thoughts. At the beginning of these meetings, there were inevitably introductions, and I easily could have shrunk into the background feeling that my résumé didn't qualify me for a seat at the table or a voice in the discussion.

At times I had to lean on my faith that Eric was a smart person and had purposefully brought me with him to contribute to the conversation, so I had to trust that I was able to add value. He would inevitably call on me after a conversation had been going on for a while, as he had done in the meeting with the king, and ask me, in front of everyone, for my reaction and clarifying questions. This was consistently terrifying, but I learned that he did so because of the value in my nonexpert observations, which could guide the conversation in a productive direction and get at the heart of the problems we were trying to solve.

While these meeting rooms and attendees were exceptional, I certainly was not. This is true for anyone wanting to expand their influence who is willing to put in the work and earn it. The pathway into these rooms where decisions are being made is long, and the preparation you will put in to qualify yourself often feels invisible. However, the results show up in your work. This will give you the confidence to raise your hand for opportunities, to be seen as contributing beyond your current job description, and to be able to drag your own chair up to bigger and bigger tables. There are never vacancies. You have to make room for yourself.

CHAPTER 5 ROI SPRINT

What opportunities already exist for you to bring your skills to a bigger table? In what ways is imposter syndrome holding you back? What squad can you create of people who are just one or two steps ahead of you and who can advise you? Who do you need to add or remove from your team in order to have your own dream team? Are there systems you can create that would benefit both your team and your own individual ambitions? Do your teammates consider you the calm in the storm? How can you use what makes you unique to claim your seat at the table of your dreams?

Recognize: What tables do you want to be sitting at? What can you uniquely offer to qualify yourself to be in the room and then at the table? Who do you need to have on your team to get you there?

Own: What will you volunteer for, research, or ask for this week that will move you one step closer to this goal?

Implement: Make the first step to pursue this plan today!

GETTING THINGS DONE

*E*mployees can do more than they realize to promote and queue themselves up for additional responsibility and visibility on their team. When you realize that there are mutually beneficial ways to ease the burdens of overworked executives and provide growth opportunities for yourself, magic starts to happen.

There are three keys to becoming and being recognized as the next crop of junior-executive talent:

- Growing your influence
- Leveling up
- Effective collaborations

GROWING YOUR INFLUENCE

Jeff Bezos had a radically impactful program for growing executive talent and injecting his values and methodology throughout the company. In my first year at Amazon, Jeff created a role called "the Shadow." The role of the Shadow, or more formally, Technical Advisor, was to be filled by a promising junior manager who would spend a year and a half at Jeff's side. This role was similar to the role of chief of staff at other companies today. The shadow was there for two reasons.

First, from the Shadow, Jeff wanted a partner with whom he could brainstorm and debate top-level company decisions who didn't have their own agendas, deliverables, or conflicting motivations. To do that, he needed someone who was in every meeting with him, copied on every email, and included in every step of the business-development process. This gave Jeff the intellectual sparring partner he needed to remain innovative and always pushing for more impact.

Second, this unprecedented experience gave the young executive the privileged opportunity to learn to be a brain-double to Jeff. The individual would learn to ask the questions Jeff would ask, anticipate his response to ideas and proposals, push back on ideas forcefully from a sound business position, and also challenge Jeff directly as a peer. Jeff not only tolerated peer review; he craved it. He sought it out. He demanded it and created an entire role around it. This partner role was focused entirely on making Jeff the best CEO he could be.

Step Outside Your Title

In 2002, Jeff's first official Shadow was Andy Jassy, who went on to lead and become the CEO of the multibillion-dollar subsidiary company he helped found, Amazon Web Services, in 2003. Andy is now, seventeen years later, named to become Jeff's successor as CEO of Amazon at the end of 2021.

Andy was an amazing Shadow. He succeeded in partnering with Jeff when many brilliant executives before had missed the mark. Jeff had experimented with the foundational idea of what became "the Shadow" with other executives earlier in the company's history, but they had all found the experiment frustrating and failed to have the impact that Jeff craved and demanded. I suspect that this difficulty came from neither Jeff nor the junior executive being fully focused and committed to the partnership. It turns out that cloning a leader isn't possible with only a part-time effort. It needed to be a full-time priority. Andy was the first to embrace this challenge effectively.

When Andy transitioned from Shadow to leading the newly created AWS team in 2003, Colin Bryar became Jeff's second Shadow. When he first started as the Shadow, Colin came to me with questions about how best to partner with Jeff and contribute effectively. Since I spent virtually every waking hour within three feet of Jeff, I had a unique opportunity to coach him through some of those questions and offer suggestions of best practices. I helped him to prepare for meetings and even walked him through what to expect from his first flight on a private jet, even though I had yet to fly on one myself.

This dynamic with Andy and Colin inspired a career-changing idea for me personally. I realized that if I could coach them in how to partner Jeff as he became the Shadow, then why couldn't I reframe my own role as a type of Shadow too? I had access to the same information, people, and resources that the Shadow did. Why not treat my whole experience in my first postcollege job, which could have easily just been an invisible, mundane role, into my own personal Jeff Bezos apprenticeship? Why not elevate the way I saw my responsibilities and, in so doing, perhaps elevate how others viewed me? I wanted to instill in myself Jeff's business instincts. I wanted to anticipate every question, challenge, and opportunity that he and the company would face.

With that new mindset, my otherwise easily overlooked job became a daily challenge in which I thrived. I now viewed my daily tasks as an opportunity for growth and learning. I no longer saw seemingly mindless tasks, such as tracking executive-action items, as unimportant. I now saw them as an unparalleled window into the inner strategy of the company, the playbook for effective executive delegation, and I treated them like a secret handbook for how Jeff led the company. I sought out opportunities to extend myself beyond the traditional expectations of my role and apply what I was learning in unexpected ways. This was not only helpful to me in my career growth but impactful for my entire team in pushing forward Jeff's priorities and anticipating future needs or impediments. This prepared me to become an effective chief of staff myself to the CEO of Google several years later.

Create a Win-Win for Growth

I later used the methodology of the Shadow when working for Marissa during my early years at Google to up-level my impact by taking as much off of her plate as I could, which gave me opportunities to stretch both my skills and my learning. Her team was growing exponentially, and her responsibilities became bigger and bigger. Soon Marissa became the face of the Product team to our users externally. While she was focused on the major deliverables and code reviews, there were other systems that no longer fit in her calendar and needed to be run on her behalf.

I started evaluating everything in our team's operating structure and looking for ways to make it more effective and efficient. One of these projects I identified was streamlining the process of evaluating speaking requests for Marissa that came in from the communications team. Before I arrived, these requests were all logged in an enormous spreadsheet, which was sent to Marissa, and then she was asked which ones she would like to do. There was little strategy when it came to which were accepted, which were declined, and which were delegated to other team members. It was also an overwhelming exercise and one that rarely felt like a priority compared to her other tasks, but I knew that getting it wrong and not being strategic in our relationship and trust building with our users could be disastrous. We needed our users to feel included and safe in the rapidly developing technologies we were creating. This required a consistent communication strategy.

I started meeting with the communications team weekly to review the press requests and prioritize the options so that we could then come to Marissa with a strategic plan for approval. This helped us whittle the list down from the overwhelming hundreds of options, which she never had the time or desire to review, and created a system that required only a few minutes of her time for quick strategy approvals and that ensured the right things were accomplished.

This then freed the communications team up to be more proactive and seek out opportunities rather than only passively reviewing what came to us. In 2007 alone, this process led to an interview on the *Today Show*, a feature article in *Marie Claire* and *Details* magazine, as well as interviews on MSNBC, NBC, ABC, Fox, and CNBC. We also focused on increasing her speaking engagements at conferences like CES, Fortune: Most Powerful Women, and DLD. With this strategic approach to press and speeches, Marissa quickly became the public face for Google products, she raised her own professional profile, and she came one step closer to her goal of being a CEO in the future.

When Marissa was booked to be on the *Today Show*, some important things changed for me as well. I honestly can't remember which of our many product launches we were promoting at the time, but I absolutely remember that that trip to New York was booked with several live television appearances between other internal and external meetings and launch-event preparations. It was a very tight schedule, and Marissa was not known for running on schedule. I was terrified that she would get off course and miss a live TV interview entirely. I decided that the only way to be sure it would all flow smoothly was if I went with her to New York and staffed her for the forty-eight-hour trip.

I was worried to ask her for approval to join her because it hadn't been part of my job responsibilities to travel and manage live launch events. I had only ever traveled with her once before, to the conference in Zurich. I was relieved when she agreed that it was a good idea to try and see if it helped her. We took a red-eye flight from San Francisco to New York and went directly to meetings upon arrival. Marissa has an amazing ability to force herself to fall asleep immediately when she needs to. This is a gift that I do not have. She is able to catnap anywhere, anytime, and is able to function at her highest level with only about four hours of sleep. I have insomnia even in perfect conditions.

When we landed in New York, she hit the ground running, and we worked a very long day. I finally collapsed in my hotel room around two o'clock in the morning and got about three hours of sleep before my alarm went off at five o'clock. We had to be at the *Today Show* by six o'clock for television-level hair and makeup and preparation. Being in the greenroom and watching the live television interview while standing behind the cameraman was a new experience for me, and it made me understand even more what Marissa's impact was for our team and company as a whole and how to deliver it. I loved the pace, the power, and the strategy of the launch-event media.

Most importantly, this experience opened my eyes and my imagination to additional ways I could help my team be successful in bringing our products to the world. I was exhausted by the end of the day but buzzing with so much energy that I couldn't even sleep on the return red-eye flight to California. Not only had this been my very first visit to New York, it was also an experience that set off a domino effect in my career and made me bold enough to ask for more of myself and to seek out projects of even greater impact. I wanted a seat at that table and in that spotlight.

After the trip to New York, I started to travel with Marissa on every work trip. We visited remote Google offices, met with CEOs of major companies, attended all of the major technology conferences, and did press events all over the United States. This prepared me to be in meeting rooms with Eric, Google's CEO, in the future, which I never would have otherwise dared dream of.

Through this shared growth focus, Marissa grew her influence as an executive and I grew mine as an individual contributor. This was the start of a very effective pattern in our work together and was a win-win for both of our careers.

LEVELING UP

The only way to learn how to speak with authority is to simply seek out and lean into situations that demand it. If you want to grow your skills, you need to prepare yourself with information, expose yourself to strategic approaches, and take on tasks that challenge your current levels of expertise to expand into new areas. I have found that when I have properly prepared, I have been able to respond to stretch projects with strength I didn't know I had.

The most important part of leveling up is taking the right kind of risks, which challenge you with tasks that you know you will not perform perfectly, out of lack of experience, but through which you will be able to learn a lot in a short amount of time. This is the kind of stress I learned to not only welcome but seek out over time.

One of these foundation-building projects for me was single-handedly building the Google Flight department. In August 2011, Google acquired Motorola for $12.5 billion. It was one of the largest acquisitions in Google history. This acquisition was very complicated, and it took a lot of executive time to determine how to maximize the value of our purchase. The Motorola purchase would enable us to advance Android through applications of their intellectual property and patents. We also had the difficult task of sorting through the employees to see where we had redundancies and determining who would remain and continue as a Google employee.

Mobile applications were a big bet for Google at the time that required a lot of risk-taking. Eric Schmidt, my manager and the CEO, had made a personal career bet on investing heavily in mobile technologies as the future upon which Google should focus and for which we should build our product platforms. The Google company OKR that year was "mobile first," which meant that every team across the company had to design for mobile optimization in everything we launched. I wanted to align my opportunities to level-up with this big bet because I knew I would receive executive support with another win-win proposal.

My part in the Motorola acquisition and chance to level-up my leadership experience took an unexpected turn. The company acquisition included all of Motorola's company assets, like their intellectual property, which motivated the purchase, as well as their employees and even their private jet fleet. Eric tasked me with the role of deciding what to do with these newly acquired jets and flight staff. Google had never owned a company jet before, although Eric and our founders owned some personal aircraft with which I had experience. I had also managed and created our executive charter jet contracts and policies, so this felt like a natural way to take that to the next level. Based on these peripheral experiences, I needed to expand my expertise into that which was needed for ownership of a fleet.

This was a project that at first felt far above my pay grade, since I had no idea what went into the maintenance, staffing, and logistics of a fleet, small or otherwise. I broke this integration project down into three parts: first, the employees; second, the aircraft; and third, building a corporate-use policy. I took on the least-pleasant task first, which was to interview all of the Motorola flight-department employees, including managers, schedulers, mechanics, pilots, and flight attendants, and decide who was essential personnel and would be a good culture fit for Google.

I quickly found that the corporate culture at Motorola was drastically different from Google's, so it was a challenge to envision most of the flight-department employees making an easy transition into their new environment. While I tasked others with evaluating their job skills, I focused on determining if they would be a good fit in the Google culture. This team was going to be fairly separate from the rest of the Google population, so there was some leeway there; however, the Googlers with whom they did interact would be our most senior executives, so they needed to present themselves in a certain way and adopt what we internally referred to as a Googley mindset, which is at the heart of the corporate culture.

Being Googley is something we talked about on a daily basis at work. This involved a certain type of creative problem-solving that was collaborative, ambitious, and highly analytical while remaining humble and not taking yourself too seriously. It takes a rare combination of top expertise and lack of ego to strike this balance. Few people can do both well. The technical expertise of this team was high. What I needed to do was see who could rise to the innovative culture of Google and teach them to shift from being a reactionary team who just follows orders to a creative team that could reinvent their team culture with me.

Expanding Your Skill Set

The first meetings with the flight-team leadership were far too formal, with stiff PowerPoint presentations (which aren't even allowed in internal Google meetings!) and a business plan that was based on hierarchy that just didn't fit our innovative and flat-management structure. There was nothing innovative or proactive in their plan at first. I knew that we needed to create something that uniquely reflected Google's value and pace of growth. It was a joy to watch a few of them perk up and really catch the vision for creating a revolutionary approach to executive travel and start brainstorming ideas with me for how we could create more efficiency and fun in their work. On the other hand, some of them immediately became uneasy, defensive of their old habits, and clearly uncomfortable with experimentation.

It was gut-wrenching for me to have to make recommendations of who to let go for the first time in my career, but I knew in my heart that those employees wouldn't be happy in this new environment and would thrive if let go to find a more traditional team. This was a struggle, but I ended up with a small, core team of partners to work with me on the next steps of evaluating the fleet and deciding which of the three jets were worth the expense of keeping.

After long analysis with the team and looking at the use cases and cost of operating each, I recommended selling one of the smaller aircraft, keeping the largest one for the long term, and keeping the second, smaller jet for a few years until the maintenance costs increased with age. I then needed to write a Google corporate-jet use policy to decide who got to use the jet when and for what purposes.

I needed to create a formula for evaluating conflicting requests and ensuring that the most critical uses were always prioritized, and that didn't always hinge on someone's seniority. There were times when a more junior executive had a much stronger use case for the jet than another more senior executive. I personally owned this approval and operational process for the first several years after the acquisition.

I created transparent, visibly published guidelines and spent extra time explaining the thought processes each time I approved or declined a request to ensure a collaborative approach that resulted in each executive feeling valued and understood. I trained their executive assistants on the policies so that they could help advocate for the right resources from the earliest planning stages and represent their best case for the jet each time. I also made sure that I always gave each executive an effective alternative solution that respected the importance of their work and reflected how Google needed to spend its resources at that moment. This careful approach avoided any unnecessary power plays or misunderstandings.

I absolutely could not have been successful in this project if I hadn't spent years building relationships of trust with these executives through my detailed understanding of Google's core strategy, priorities, and deliverables to shareholders. I had spent years building up watertight relationships of trust with them. Only with that foundation could I manage up to these executives in a way that empowered them even when I had to tell them no.

My job description for most of my career could be summarized this way: I told people no for a living while making them feel good about it. That was the art of it.

A common mistake is to only see growth value in projects that seem glamorous or sit firmly in the spotlight. Most of my career advancements have come by doing projects that no one else wanted to do. Running the Google Flight department involved a lot of late nights studying FAA policies so I could be sure we were compliant, talking with aviation attorneys, researching tax implications for the company and our executives, and assisting with last-minute plane swapping due to changing company priorities. This was a full-time job that I had to figure out how to do so efficiently that it could be done as a side project in my already-full day. These unglamorous tasks built up my reputation as someone who is proactive, collaborative, and indispensable for getting the right things done for the company. These opportunities are available at any career level when you actively look for them.

It's also tempting to only seek out the exciting projects that are fun and that give visibility but don't contribute at the base level where the team really needs dedicated attention. Ego can be our worst enemy in development. Humility is a core value of truly innovative people and ironically is an essential ingredient in learning to speak with authority.

In general, this approach has worked out for me. When you focus on contributing things of value, inevitably you get noticed, and you can thereby create your own good luck and unexpected opportunities.

Being Scrappy

A large part of learning to speak with new authority comes from reframing your contributions, both in your own mind and in the minds of those to whom you report.

In the summer of 2012, Google was invited to attend the London Olympics by the International Olympic Committee (IOC). While Eric had attended several Olympic Games before, this relationship had become particularly strategic for the company that year. Our YouTube Sports division had been in long negotiations with the IOC for permission to broadcast Olympic content. The traditional broadcasting model gave exclusive broadcasting rights to a single major network for each country. However, having only one content partner meant that the amount of airtime was limited to only major sports and that the other athletes never received any airtime. We wanted them to get the airtime they deserved and to offer additional mentors and inspiration for young athletes across the globe in more diverse sports.

Google could take the content that networks didn't broadcast and make the rest available online. This would protect their existing contracts as well as expand their audience and bring in younger viewers, who were moving away from traditional TV viewing experiences. The IOC is slow to adapt to newer business models, so our conversations continued across the following two Olympics, in Sochi, Russia, and Seoul, Korea, as well. This was a welcomed project for me given my lifelong obsession with the Olympics and the astounding athletes who competed in them.

It was a bewildering experience to attend the Olympics for the first time. Thankfully I had the forsight to arrive a few days in advance of the team to test out how things worked with our badges and security clearances. Every stadium, event, and room seemed to require a different authorization badge. The IOC had given me the lowest-possible special-access badge, which meant that I couldn't enter most of the rooms where the meetings between Google and the Olympic Committee would be taking place, which meant that I could not do the job that the company had sent me to the other side of the world to do. I wouldn't be able to access the Olympic transportation service between venues or get into the meeting rooms in order to drive our collaboration, and it was up to me to find a work-around.

I realized quickly that I needed to make Karen, the IOC's logistics coordinator for VIPs, my very best friend. I wasn't able to convince her to give me full access, but she gave enough for me to be allowed to use the exclusive executive car service, so that I could ride with the team and review the briefings before each meeting as well as enter the secure areas within the venues where the meetings were taking place. It did not, however, allow me to sit down. Literally. I was not allowed a seat in any stadium, event space, or meeting room. It was hilariously awkward, but at least I could do my job. And I was at the Olympics, for goodness sake!

It wasn't easy work, but I loved every second of it. Every morning I woke up early to test the travel routes we would need to take because each location had its own specific entrance and security procedures, and sometimes it could take me a full hour, which we didn't have to spare in the schedule, just to figure this out.

In the evenings, I would meet with the YouTube Sports leadership team to review all of the takeaways from that day's meetings, and we would create follow-up briefings and devise and divide up the action items for each. This would go late into the night, and then we would sleep for a few hours before doing it all over again. When all was said and done, I was fortunate enough, thanks to Eric's personal generosity, to be able to stay a few days in London and attend several Olympic events so that I could finally have a seat and witness the greatest athletes in the world for myself.

Flexing Your Grit

I was in awe of just how spectacular these athletes were and yet how normal their beginnings and family lives often were. They had to learn at a very young age to own their authority and expertise as elite athletes. I sat and watched the swimming heats next to the families of these athletes, who had clearly poured their hearts and souls into supporting them.

I sat in the row behind the parents of Ryan Lochte as he added more medals to his collection to become the second-most decorated swimmer of all time. I also sat next to the family of a Japanese swimmer who had no chance of winning a medal but who had made his dream come true of becoming an Olympian. As a family, they had all sacrificed so many other pleasures in pursuit of this seemingly impossible task. The athletes themselves had lost sleep, sacrificed paychecks, kept strict diets, enjoyed limited free time with friends, and performed tirelessly over and over and over again while seeking perfection and microsecond improvements that could mean the difference between winning and losing on the world stage.

I enjoyed talking to the families of these athletes as much as I enjoyed watching Michael Phelps swim what was then his farewell competition and break the all-time medal record. What struck me most about all of these athletes' stories was how they all had dealt with seemingly insurmountable failures and setbacks. They had all suffered major injuries, loss of coaches, struggles with funding, and other things that could have derailed them entirely from their dreams. But they all stubbornly fought back to make their dreams a reality despite all odds to become champions.

I learned that there are many correlations between athletic success and business success: First, you need to be bold enough to dare to dream of having your name up in lights in a stadium or on the door of the CEO's office. Second, you need to be stubborn enough to not give up when you suffer an injury or run out of funding and to not listen to your critics. Third, you need to be humble enough to be able to listen to wise coaches and mentors who challenge you to rise to a higher level of greatness when you are already performing better than 99 percent of your competition. And, most importantly, you need to have your compass and confidence come from a place deep inside yourself that does not need the validation of others.

I recently asked a colleague of mine who is a professional championship soccer player in the UK what it is like when people wear his jersey and what it is like to go into a stadium where people chant his name when he steps onto the field. He wisely replied that you cannot let that affect you. If you do, you are as likely to be affected when the entire stadium boos you for making a mistake or missing a shot. I have made my fair share of humiliating mistakes at work and often in front of people who are very powerful and senior to me, but I have never actually been booed. Can you imagine being booed by tens of thousands of people? He is right, of course. If my self-worth had been tied to the opinions and validation of others, I would never have been able to survive long enough to later exceed their expectations.

The same people who cheer for you one day can sometimes hold you back the next when you make a mistake, even though mistakes are a necessary part of your learning and development. I have had to bet on myself, self-validate as I learn, and measure my progress internally. It is a challenge to have this champion's mentality, but I try to live in that zone as much as I can.

I wish I could say that my business contributions during that first Olympic experience in London were great, but the truth is that I learned a lot of things the hard way through a lot of wasted time and energy and with tired, sore feet. There were a lot of things that I wasn't prepared for and hadn't anticipated. And honestly, I couldn't have learned them any other way; I just had to show up and struggle through it.

I tried to focus my frustrations productively and dedicate time while at the Olympic Games to building up very strong friendships with the major decision makers as well as learning how to navigate the politics and antiquated ways in which business got done there. I wasted so much time being locked outside of venue doors, but I always figured out ways to get my tasks accomplished otherwise. And, most importantly, I figured out what to ask for so that I could be more effective the next time. These challenges were analogous to my entire career progression.

When we went to the Olympic Games in Russia and South Korea to do it all again, I knew exactly the kind of security badges we needed, what match tickets I needed to request in advance, and the best places for our team to orchestrate hallway chats with world leaders, celebrities, and dignitaries so that we were always in the right place at the right time. That took years of experimentation and relationship building to perfect.

There are more commonalities than differences between athletes, top CEOs, and champions of any kind. They all learn to own their power step-by-step and line-by-line through calculated risk-taking, braving embarrassments, and consistently pushing the boundaries of their abilities. This is how you become a dominant force. This is how you speak with authority just by entering a room.

EFFECTIVE COLLABORATIONS

The best way to invest in yourself is to take full advantage of opportunities to work on cross-collaborative projects, no matter how small they may seem. These projects build both skills and relationships across the organization. I have been amazed at how taking on seemingly small and unimportant projects has allowed me to build up relationships that provide career-changing opportunities down the road. This is a pattern that has repeated itself over and over across my career.

During my first year at Google, I realized quickly that the only way I would be truly effective in my work at the company was if

I built up relationships beyond my core team. Relationships were a huge part of how things got done at Google before we had all the documented procedures and systems in place that exist today. I decided that I needed to work on a cross-functional project to build up my network and project-management skills.

Becoming Mission Control

Marissa and Sheryl Sandberg, while they were both still executives at Google, decided to host the first-ever Women@Google talk, which would become a continuing series at the company. This was a way for them to establish their thought leadership both inside and outside the company as female executives and to create a dialogue around important issues. This first edition would be with Jane Fonda and Gloria Steinem. I raised my hand immediately to take the lead. I had no idea how to do this and I had absolutely no spare time in which to do it, but I realized that this was a chance to learn how to get things done at Google after months of struggling to work effectively alone.

I accidentally stepped on a few toes before I discovered that there was a grassroots Talks@Google team of volunteer Googlers who hosted talks with authors, celebrities, scientists, and more. They walked me through hosting my first event and all the complexities involved with coordinating external guests, security, advertising, book buying, and the AV team.

The talk was a success by all definitions. Marissa and Sheryl were established successfully as thought leaders, and my mission to make some friends across several teams in the company and to have some resources to call upon for huge projects in the future was accomplished.

I joined the Talks@Google team as one of the original ten members and participated in it all twelve years I was at the company. Through this side project, I learned how to manage every aspect of producing major live events and made countless mistakes on the way to perfecting the process. Some of our early successes in hosting these talks made me pivot and learn quickly from some logistical mistakes.

After one very popular talk I hosted with the comedian Conan O'Brien, which resulted in a flood of over a thousand eager employees lined up for hours outside the event space, hoping for one of the few hundred seats inside, I worked with the internal communications team to create systems for managing high-demand events without wasting the very expensive time of our employees. I set up a lottery system for getting a seat inside the venue in advance and then, in collaboration with our YouTube team, we created an online streaming option so that those who didn't receive a seat could watch from their desks and so we could broadcast these exclusive events for free to our users.

Over the next decade, I personally organized and hosted the companywide talks for Barack Obama, Tina Fey, Hillary Clinton, and Stephen Colbert. This became one of my favorite perks of working at Google and my most effective way of building up my network across the company. I was inspired by my frequent, direct exposure to some of the most influential people in the world, all while making opportunities for myself and the company as well.

The most memorable of these events was when we hosted a series of talks by the major presidential candidates during the 2008 election, which we then posted on our Talks@Google YouTube channel, so voters across the United States could watch and become informed. Candidates Barack Obama, Hillary Clinton, and John McCain were interviewed individually by Eric onstage. I coordinated the Secret Service campus sweeps in advance, and I was thrilled to be able to personally give Senator Obama a quick campus tour and familiarize him with our unique work culture before he took the stage.

These cross-collaborative efforts were helpful both to me individually and presented opportunities for the company's success for years to come in unexpected ways.

When Barack Obama was elected president of the United States, our offices started coordinating and meeting regularly. I will never forget the day that Eric and I went to the White House, several years after hosting Obama for the first time at Google, for policy meetings and relationship building.

The experience was exactly like you see in the movies. Our car was searched at the security checkpoint, and we went through several screening stations outside the building before being allowed in. We were given security badges that were color coded for our security clearance level and then walked to reception.

The receptionist at the main desk for the West Wing that day was a woman who was deaf. She had an interpreter who partnered with her in answering the phones and managing the arriving executives and dignitaries. I loved watching the way they worked together, completely in sync. I was distracted—I kept looking around in the lobby trying to savor every detail of this unique experience—and I was embarrassed to be the last to notice that I needed to rise to my feet before Charles, Prince of Wales, walked out of the West Wing and exited through the door next to me. We were up next.

After meeting with President Obama's personal secretary, Ferial Govashiri, she kindly asked me if I would like to go into the Oval Office. Obviously! I will never forget entering the Oval

Office or the feeling of its plush, cream-colored carpet. I touched Obama's desk and felt the history that had been made in that room. The desk had been a gift from Queen Victoria in 1880 to President Rutherford B. Hayes and had been used by Presidents John F. Kennedy and Jimmy Carter as well. As an American woman, literally born on a US Air Force base, this was a significant moment.

I had lunch in the outer Oval Office, just two feet outside that room, with Obama's staff. That moment made me reflect on how seemingly small things, if you're willing to put in the work, can qualify you to join the disrupters and leaders of the world.

Far too many people get distracted by fancy titles and seemingly prestigious projects and forget to play the long game. I have so many friends whose big breaks in their careers came from someone with whom they spent an internship a decade earlier. Invest in your relationships and cast your net wide by getting to know as many people and skills as possible.

Once you have cross-functional skills firmly in your toolbelt, a fast-track to promotion and to building senior-level relationships is to find opportunities where you can partner with an executive a level or two above you on a project that neither of you has done before. This is how you become a core part of mission control. This puts both of you on a more even playing field and removes barriers that otherwise would naturally exist between your responsibilities. It is also essential to remain humble, teachable, and collaborative, or you can unwittingly limit your own growth potential and alienate the very people with whom you are trying to build respect.

Uniting Through Disruption

In 2012, Eric wanted to do something a little disruptive while we were in the early stages of our newly created roles at Google—him as executive chairman and me as chief of staff. I jumped at the chance to collaborate on a project that would be new for us both and would allow us to share ideas and brainstorm together. It was a rare opportunity.

Eric wanted to create a conference that was unlike any other. He had spent twenty-plus years of his career attending the same conferences with "the same group of old white guys, saying the same things," year after year. We envisioned a conference where experts from all kinds of industries and the most influential people in the world could gather and discuss ideas without any more of an agenda than smart people connecting with smart people in the hopes that world-changing projects would naturally follow these newly formed relationships.

This became an annual event. Eric invited five of his closest colleagues to cohost the event with him and select the attendees. The attendees included the world's best and most influential people from a variety of industries, including journalists, authors, heads of state, economists, scientists, photographers, artists, musicians, and filmmakers, all of whom had received the highest prizes offered in their respective fields.

In the conference sessions, we would discuss current events, debate global policies, and, most importantly, forge new, cross-disciplinary friendships that wouldn't have happened otherwise. These connections would lead to collaborative projects for global good for years to come. While this was an enormous undertaking to put together, it felt worth the long hours and stress for the opportunity to create something that could impact the real world for the better.

Putting together an event like this from scratch took an enormous amount of time, project-management skills, and patience from my entire team. The first year, we hired an event coordinator who had managed an external conference that Eric had often attended in the past; he was always very impressed with how it was managed. We brought her on as a contractor to implement his vision of a modern "un-conference."

I had been really excited to work with her and learn from her experience and leadership within the elite-conference skill set. Unfortunately, she was not a good culture fit for our team from the start, and this created a lot of stress and frustration for everyone involved. She came from a corporate culture of siloed information, strict hierarchy, and lack of trust and transparency. Google is highly collaborative, open with ideas and suggestions, and fiercely flat in management structure.

While the Googlers, as employees are called, shared brainstorming documents, contact lists, and project-management tracking sheets, this contractor refused to share any of her work product, and we were constantly out of sync. She wanted to be the only one to present ideas to Eric, which is not his style of leadership, nor mine. She kept everything tightly in her vault, which made it impossible for anyone else to contribute effectively. The team felt constantly disrespected and unvalued, and our contributions were diminished.

The first year's conference was a huge success from the attendee perspective, but it was hard for those of us who had put it together to feel fully proud. I was certainly just relieved that the stress and the conflict of it was over. That experience was a master class in how not to run a team project and how important it is to adapt to the culture and values of the organization you are serving.

From then on, we managed the conference internally, without an external event coordinator, and the experience of planning, as well as the results, were like night and day. It was so fun to feel disruptive not only in the unique event we were producing but also in the way we all worked together.

Even the attendees who had enjoyed the first year's event commented on the incredible improvements in the experience the second year. Our work reflected that we all respected and valued each other and that our individual talents had contributed to the value of the whole. It was a joy to work on it, even though it meant many late nights and meticulous planning.

Most technology companies are known for being systematically innovative because of two main factors. First, they often have a clear company mission and vision communicated from senior management, and second, they often have unencumbered channels for ideas to flow from the bottom up. This is why the contractor's methods were met with such resistance from our collaborative Google team. The best ideas often come from the newest employees because they have the advantage of looking at the company mission and their own deliverables without the burden of seeing things through the lens of "the way that things have always been done." Fresh eyes can offer creative, innovative solutions that more experienced team members often cannot.

While our team worked incredibly well together, it was not free from frustrations or growing pains. As the years progressed, I wanted to move from my role of overseeing the complex logistics side of the event to one that contributed more substantially to the agenda content as well as curating the guest list. I first focused on submitting names of possible attendees who I thought could uniquely contribute to the goal of the event and who came from more diverse backgrounds of expertise, seniority, gender, religion, or region; I wanted to bring currently underrepresented voices into the conversation and experience. I also tried to offer topic suggestions that I thought needed global attention.

While I was always treated with respect, I was disappointed that I felt actively thwarted by some members of our planning group who wanted to retain that control and stay firmly within their personal Rolodex. I have always taken a team approach, so I let these slights go. I tried year after year to contribute substantially to the mission of the conference with agendas and unique voices, but I felt like I failed to make a truly meaningful dent in that area. I think the culture of year one permeated the foundation, and I wasn't able to break down those barriers despite my best efforts.

This was a rare experience for me at Google and is one I still view as a failure on my part. Over the seven years I helped run this event, only three of my attendee suggestions were offered an invitation, and none of my agenda topics were adopted. This meant that I did not reach my personal goal to diversify the attendee demographics or session themes effectively, which was a core part of this conference's inception. We remained too similar to the conferences we were trying to replace, the ones with the "same old white guys" talking. This was the first moment when I started to realize that my next growth steps might need to happen outside of Google. It took five more years before I made that leap.

Even with a firm culture of collaboration in a company, there can be unintended roadblocks that need to be actively removed. Leaders and core contributors need to constantly question their practices, policies, and habits to be sure they are cultivating, encouraging, and forging a natural path for rising stars in their organization.

CHAPTER 6 ROI SPRINT

What are ways in which you can step outside your traditional job description and invite new, cross-collaborative projects? Is there a way to create a win-win where you remove a burden from your team or manager that will give you a chance to grow a new skill or take the lead in a new way? How can you expand your skill set and adopt a championship mindset that isn't derailed even as you make mistakes through the learning process? Is there a way for you to gain critical skills or expertise that will qualify you to become part of mission control? Are there inefficiencies that you could address through creative disruption?

Recognize: What opportunities are there for you to increase your influence within your company or industry? How can you collaborate with someone at a different seniority level in a way that will benefit you both?

Own: Which stakeholders can you talk to this week for sign-off on a cross-functional project?

Implement: Create a documented growth plan with your manager that will expose you to new teams, projects, skills, and expertise. This will advance your career and get you noticed.

PURPOSEFUL
RISK-TAKING

I first experienced the power of bold risk-taking when working for Jeff Bezos at Amazon in the early 2000s, while he was not only inventing the gold standard of e-commerce but also literally building rocket ships. However, it wasn't until I worked at Google that I truly caught the vision for the moonshot process: I saw it while sitting with the Google X team one day a week for over a decade and watching them invent the technologies that will power our future lives.

Google X, now renamed simply X, is in a building that used to be a shopping mall several decades ago. Rather than building it out as an office space with the signature vibrantly colored and expertly designed interiors of the other global Google buildings, Sergey Brin instructed the design team to keep it bare-bones and tactical. The walls are few and the structure is mostly bare concrete columns, with the original engineering spray paint markings and electrical and fiber cables cascading down from the ceilings. It is cold yet full of energy and movement, like an airplane hangar. There are wires and mockups and parts strewn around full-scale models of cars, lasers, cameras, weather balloons, and unidentifiable contraptions everywhere you look. The staircases twist through the open atrium in the middle of the building, connecting all the mad scientists as if in a black-and-white Dr. Seuss book. The energy is palpable.

The senior-leadership strategy-team meetings were moved from Google's main campus to this building as a conscious effort to be sure that the senior leadership was exposed to a blank-slate environment and primed for innovative thinking. The SVP's direct reports, including me, camped outside the conference room in a large open area with tall tables we used as standing desks. We swarmed around like a beehive all day, exchanging ideas, catching up, planning, and collaborating. It was such a productive change of pace and environment that we started to hold our quarterly board of directors meeting there as well. This is how we tried to remain innovative, creative, and disruptive of even our own previous best practices.

My career has surrounded me with people who lean into and actively seek out this kind of industry disruption, and I have learned how they stomach not only the daily ambiguity of trying to create something that doesn't yet exist, but also the required constant cycle of failure that informs their next steps.

The truth is that the same formula that has helped X invent world-changing technologies, such as driverless cars, can also be applied to individual lives and career ambitions. Malcolm X famously said that "the future belongs to those who prepare for it today." While he was talking specifically about the civil rights movement in the United States in 1962, this principle can be applied broadly. If we want a future that offers exceptional opportunities, then we need to take action early rather than accept the easy road. These future opportunities often never come without decisive action well in advance.

I learned early on that I cannot passively wait for opportunities to make my dreams come true. I had to qualify myself for a seat at future tables by doing the groundwork today to learn and gain the experience necessary to contribute at that level. An unavoidable aspect of this qualification process is failure.

During my two decades working at Amazon and Google, I have seen repeatedly that there are three key elements to creating our own future moonshot opportunities:

- Be an infinite learner.
- Seek out things that make you uncomfortably excited.
- Make big bets early.

The greatest predictor of future success is one's willingness to learn, experiment, fail, and repeat until one can produce the desired effect predictably. The challenge of learning new skills and mastering them is a reward in and of itself, but it also qualifies us for higher achievements the next time.

My work philosophy has always been that my job should give as much to me as I give to it. And that is a decidedly high bar! What I give in terms of time, effort, and risk-taking should be rewarded with learning, skill, growth, and empowered advancement. The secret is that I had to take charge and demand this exchange. It did not happen automatically or passively. It is up to me to know what I want to learn and who I want to become and then seek it out.

BE AN
INFINITE LEARNER

It is no accident that Jeff is one of the most successful CEOs of our time. Yes, he has spectacular natural talent, intelligence, and drive. What differentiates him is the way he cultivates these abilities. When I worked at Amazon, I organized a weeklong thinking retreat for him every quarter. This had been a practice of his from long before I arrived. He would go to a hotel nearby and lock himself away from his usual routine, his staff, and his family. The first few days were spent starving himself of outside influences like newspapers, books, television, or people.

Jeff explained to me that he needed to craft a period of time to clear his mind of clutter and noise before he could open space in his mind for innovative ideas to enter. Boredom was an essential part of his creative process. The only things he brought with him were blank notebooks and a pen. The second half of the week he spent filling the notebook with free-flowing, unedited ideas. He would come back to the office the following week with notebooks filled with industry-changing ideas and strategies that we would spend the following quarter implementing.

The remarkable thing was that Jeff often stepped away for these retreats during our most critical growth moments of the company, when others might have been tempted to double down on their hours in the office and conference rooms. Jeff was wise enough to know that his greatest asset was his mind, and he needed to create a place where he could fully tap into his inner strength and ingenuity. When he returned to the office, his productivity was always at an all-time high, and he more than made up for the hours he had spent away from the office.

Even now, nearly two decades later, I smile when I watch Amazon launching things that were born on those thinking retreats so long ago, ideas documented in those notebooks.

I have implemented my own versions of a thinking retreat across the different stages of my career. In my early years it wasn't reasonable to expect the company to give me a week off every quarter just to think. In truth, at the earliest stages of my career, I rarely protected even having a lunch break for myself, but that was a shortsighted error. I finally realized that balance and taking care of myself was the best way to ensure I remained a valuable asset.

One of the greatest lessons I learned from working for Marissa, while we were averaging 100–130 hours a week, was to focus on what she called "finding your rhythm." She would actively ask her direct reports what they needed in order not to feel resentful of their demanding workload. For example, one of Marissa's direct reports was a mother to three young children. She didn't mind managing a critical project in Bangalore that required her to have regular video meetings at two o'clock in the morning as long as she could have dinner and bedtime with her kids first. She valued being both an active mom to her kids *and* owning one of the most strategic growth projects in the company. That was her rhythm. Once Marissa knew what each team member valued and filled them up outside of work, she became the biggest defender of that time. This wasn't exactly work/life balance but it was a rhythm that allowed each person to keep pace and feel happy for the long haul.

With this permission in place, I created rituals for myself that built me up and gave me the resilience I needed to sustain the demanding pace. For the first time, I prioritized taking care of myself. I made it nonnegotiable to have time to work out for an hour every single morning. I needed to consistently move my body in order to tap into the most creative, problem-solving part of my brain. Later in my career, when I became a manager, I started to set boundaries around my work hours so that I could unplug and insisted that my team do the same. I even set a team OKR that we all set a specific hobby outside of work that would create this rhythm we each needed in order to recharge.

Today, as an entrepreneur where I have more freedom over how my time is spent, I have extended my morning routine beyond the daily workout and set aside an hour every morning for free-flowing inspiration, during which I normally read articles or books or listen to podcasts, and a second hour during which I note thoughts, ideas, and systems I want to implement in my company or in those of my clients. Having this ritual every morning allows me to start each day with an open mind and innovative problem-solving approach. This consistent investment in myself has been game-changing!

The Learning Mindset

Jeff was a daily example to me of the importance of being purposeful and aware of your mindset and making sure that it isn't fixed, although not once during my years at Amazon did I hear anyone talk about mindset. This was learned purely by example. It was still a few years before Carol Dweck published her foundational book, *Mindset: The New Psychology of Success*, which provided a framework for me to understand what I had witnessed in Jeff's world-changing way of approaching life and business. What I saw modeled in his daily choices and patterns helped me evolve my way of thinking and approach toward my life and career as a risk-taker despite my timid nature.

Because working for Jeff at Amazon was my first job after graduating from college, I arrived still firmly entrenched with a performance mindset: my goals and motivations were based on the expectation of performing well (like acing an exam in school) as a means to winning praise, being compared favorably to my peers, and thus motivating me further to perform better. But what I noticed in Jeff and my colleagues at Amazon was that this was a limiting mindset. While a performance mindset was important in my goal-setting and growth tracking, it was also making me shy away from taking risks out of fear of not performing perfectly.

I realized that if I tried to avoid new projects out of a fear of not performing well, I would miss out on the greatest joys of working at a company like Amazon and rob myself of discovering new talents and sharpening still-rough skills—all while depriving myself of fully enjoying the wild ride of being smack at the center of the early years of creating modern e-commerce!

I confess: I can still be seduced by the performance mindset. As a perfectionist, my greatest fear has been looking stupid in front of people whose opinions I care about. Over my career, I've learned that I don't need to mind what absolutely everyone around me thinks. The only opinions that actually matter are mine and those of a few key stakeholders. That's it.

Jeff exemplified a learning mindset. In fact, "learn and be curious" is one of Amazon's fourteen leadership principles by which employees are measured. He prioritized opportunities to learn as much as he could from every task and person around him. In all of Jeff's meetings, he required a thorough agenda in advance as well as a written report of the topic and researched recommendations for course of action, which everyone would read to themselves at the start of the meeting. PowerPoint presentations were literally banned. These written reports needed to satisfy

Jeff's obsession with data-driven decision-making. The reports removed the chances of being swayed by a charismatic presenter rather than facts and active debates. It is also much more challenging to write a six-page memo, which became the longest length allowed, than it is a twenty-slide PowerPoint deck because it requires you to have a much deeper understanding of the issues involved and a fully fleshed out argument. The PowerPoint ban for meetings is common practice at Google and other tech companies as well for the same reasons.

This process of preparation ensured that the executives at the table were presented with the facts needed to make educated decisions and calculated risks. We adopted this approach in our team meetings when presenting to Jeff, as his SVPs did. Each question we presented to him was accompanied by a thoroughly researched, proposed course of action for discussion and approval. This way we were never presenting Jeff with a list of problems—we were focused on discovering and proposing *solutions*.

I learned that the benefit of doing your homework, forming your own opinion, and having your voice heard far outweighs the fear of making a mistake. It took me a few months to get over the hesitation of possibly making the wrong recommendation to Jeff in our daily team meetings. My fear wasn't unfounded. Jeff never holds back if he thinks you haven't thought something through or done something properly. His comments can really cut you to the core, if you let them. You have to quickly develop a thick skin to work effectively with him and not allow his challenges to dissolve your confidence. In the end, the comments, no matter how hard they are to hear, make you a better thinker.

Turn Learning into Action

In my early career, my self-inflicted homework alone was not enough. I had to actually take action on what I had learned intellectually through studying and research. Looking back, I can see now that most of my growth at Amazon came from volunteering for things well outside my job description. For example, I helped coordinate the logistics of Jeff's participation in the launch event for the Amazon jewelry shop with Paris Hilton, who was at the height of her fame and had just released her own jewelry line. I also got a glimpse of a role into the launch of the Amazon sporting goods page, including a media event in Grand Central Terminal in New York with the tennis star Anna Kournikova, who had just endorsed a sports bra with the slogan "Only the ball should bounce."

Surely no one remembers my contributions to these early launches; the tasks I volunteered for were mostly invisible. But to me, this was invaluable exposure to how to put together a global event, how to coordinate a cross-department project, how the operational processes work to allow for global expansions, and how the work we were doing in the CEO suite was directly related to what we were able to offer our customers.

That connection fueled me as a junior employee and team member to get involved at a deeper level. Yes, this often meant signing up for some eighteen-hour days and extremely stressful situations, but it felt worth it when I saw how much I was learning that couldn't be gained any other way. If I was passive and stayed within the traditional boundaries of my role, many once-in-a-lifetime opportunities would pass me by.

I decided to make risk-taking a pattern in my work. I repeated this pattern when I joined Google and created a much larger role for myself than my title implied possible, and I had an impact in global product launches that otherwise would have never been entrusted to me.

I had to learn not to be afraid that my ideas might first be met with confused silence—which happened a lot. I realized that it was up to me to show people how to think of me, especially in my early career. This is a process that takes time and consistent effort, which can be the hardest part. It's hard to be consistently brave. But over time, when my teammates saw that I was constantly adding value, my opinions soon were not only tolerated but eventually sought out. Being willing to endure the long path of changing the perception of my value-add was the hardest part.

I knew early on that I wanted to be seen as a thought leader who is creative, fearless, and resourceful, even when I was the junior-most person in the room.

The truth I eventually discovered is that if you are always the smartest person in the room, you are in the wrong room! There is no room for growth left for you there! That is when you need to bravely leave and drag your chair up to the next table.

I have learned to always say yes to an invitation, even, or especially if, it makes me very uncomfortable and to seize opportunities that will expand my horizons.

I have been in rooms with all types of global experts, including Nobel Prize–winning scientists, heads of nations, and celebrities. In my decade working for Eric, I saw him consistently adding his insatiable curiosity, respect, and humility to each conversation. I decided that I needed to do the same in order to reach my potential.

Eric had a plaque on his desk at Google that read, "If at all possible, say yes," and he lives that to the fullest every single day. This mantra isn't about working yourself as hard as possible. It is about valuing learning experiences above all else, including your comfort zone. Eric is willing to try anything, go anywhere, and talk to anyone who will open him up to new perspectives. He does not allow potential discomfort or embarrassment to be part of the decision-making equation. I decided that this motto gave me permission to do the same.

Eric is always looking for ways to learn and level-up by doing things he has never done before, and he is often restless for a new adventure. But because he has a long history of this behavior, it can be hard for him to find things that he has never done before. A good example of this is the fact that before becoming the CEO of Google, he realized that as an executive he would be living his life on a plane. He decided that if he was going to spend his life on a jet, he might as well do the fun part, which is flying it. So he studied and completed pilot training and worked his way up to being a fully certified jet pilot on several aircraft.

Now when he flies for work, he almost always flies his private jet for at least takeoff and landing, to keep his skills sharp. It was consistently amazing to me to be with him in a tough negotiation meeting, drive to the airport, board the plane, and have him turn left and sit down in the cockpit to fly us to the next country while I turned right and prepared for our next meetings upon arrival. Eric would come to the back midflight to review the briefing documents with me, and then he would return to the cabin to make the landing.

Eventually, flying jets wasn't enough of a challenge for Eric, so he decided to also learn to fly a helicopter. Now this is where I drew the line, given my bad helicopter experiences with Jeff Bezos! I told him that I would quit if he was going to be flying helicopters, but he called my bluff and did it anyway. Whenever he was at helicopter training or doing another certification exam,

I would be a nervous wreck all day. I am certain that my nail marks are still in the back seat armrest of his helicopter from the first time he flew me for the seven-minute flight from Manhattan to Teterboro Airport.

Applied Learning

In 2013, about a year after Eric had become certified as a helicopter pilot, our team took a tour of six African countries to meet with their heads of state and discuss ways in which we could help prepare them to benefit from the online global economy. We called this project "The Next Billion Users."

We estimated that approximately a billion people living in third-world countries were about to come online for the first time, and we wanted to be sure that Google built products with these communities in mind. Almost all of these new internet users were coming online through mobile without having experienced desktops or laptops. That entrance to technology would only last them so long before they would need a more advanced internet connection because the mobile applications being designed required higher bandwidth than the old systems were able to provide.

We wanted to encourage the leaders of these developing countries to invest in the physical infrastructure needed to create an online economy for their people. We encouraged them to lay down fiber cables for fast, accessible Wi-Fi connections while they were installing water, sewer, and power lines. This would not only provide more internet users for Google; it would also offer these populations new access to information, education, and the digital economy.

Google has an office in Nairobi, and there were about twenty employees working there at the time. We started out our work in the Google office getting to know the employees there and hearing about their particular challenges, projects, and goals. From there we went to a local university and spoke to them about the future of entrepreneurship and the work Google was doing to support start-ups in Kenya.

Our entire visit was centered around learning and experiencing as much as possible. I did not want this to feel like a token tour or to merely observe the situation. I realized that I would need to allow myself to get uncomfortable and start asking questions, offering observations, and instigating delicate discussions in order to actually hope to make a difference. At first it was very uncomfortable for me because I wanted to be respectful and I had no idea how to solve the complex issues of developing these nations. I had to literally force myself to speak within the first five minutes of a meeting just to get over the fear. But once I did so, everyone in the room relaxed. My unique voice changed the meetings from feeling like one with Eric, one of the wealthiest and most powerful people in the world, to a conversation of peers wanting to do the right thing. It turned out that my more-junior status to everyone in the room was actually a strength rather than a weakness.

The perspectives we gained from these interactions changed our entire approach to our global work in the years that followed. While we were in Africa, we wanted to see how remote villages were using mobile technology, so we went to visit a community near the Maasai Mara. We were able to access this village because of Eric's helicopter-pilot skills, and we landed in the middle of their hand-built mud huts and goat herds. They welcomed us with gifts of beaded necklaces they had made themselves, and they even killed and cooked a goat in honor of our visit. They were shocked when I went with the men as they talked and because I was there when the goat was killed. Normally this is something that women were not allowed to do. I was so used to being the only woman that I hadn't noticed when the others split off.

This was the first of many isolated villages we visited across Africa, and it was amazing to see the ways in which they incorporated ancient practices with modern technologies. In remote communities across Kenya, Rwanda, South Sudan, Chad, Côte d'Ivoire, and Nigeria, we saw villages sharing a single mobile phone for access to weather information to inform their harvesting timing, medical information to replicate inaccessible doctors, and education tools to train their young students, especially girls, who did not have access to traditional schools. I was blown away by their ingenuity, creativity, resourcefulness, and natural entrepreneurial spirit.

Since that experience, whenever I feel myself stagnating in my career, I ask myself how much of my time is currently spent in my comfort zone. Am I only sitting in rooms where I already have authority? I then literally look through my calendar and task list and do the math. I have found that if I am spending more than 80 percent of my time doing tasks in which I am an overall expert and I feel comfortable knowing all the answers, then I know it's time to level-up. It is time to take on the next challenge and get myself uncomfortably excited again.

SEEK OUT THINGS THAT MAKE YOU UNCOMFORTABLY EXCITED

I have witnessed some of the greatest leaders of all time in their early years of development, and let me reassure you that their paths were not as linear toward success as they appear in retrospect. But one of the things they all have in common is their commitment to being infinite learners.

Every morning I would walk through the lobby of Building 42 between the display of original servers Larry Page and Sergey Brin built in the Stanford dorms in 1996 on my way up to the C-suite on the second floor. Whenever I had guests come to campus, I would always start the tour there so they could see where Google was born. These prized servers remain in their original case, built of Legos and insulated with old sheets of cardboard. They were a daily reminder to me of how just two people bravely set out to change the entire world. We kept this grad school mentality of constantly questioning, learning, pivoting, and delivering in action every day.

Dare to Be Unconventional

In 2004, two years before I joined Google, Larry wrote the Founders' IPO Letter as "'An Owner's Manual' for Google's Shareholders." The opening lines were easy for me to commit to memory early in my tenure as an employee because they were repeated nearly daily in the course of my work. It begins, "Google is not a conventional company. We do not intend to become one." I become emotional each time I read that letter because it was a mission statement that each employee embodied by his or her work every single day in those early years, and it is a motto I try to honor now within my own post-Google venture.

The Google founders recognized early the essential need to intentionally teach people what to expect of them. This is how they attracted the right investors to support the journey they were embarking upon, which wouldn't resemble any other.

I remain committed to, as Larry described in that letter, "develop[ing] services that significantly improve the lives of as many people as possible" through my work. When I worked at Google, every day felt like it mattered. Each project had the real possibility to make the world a better place, which was also something the letter promised. That feeling of responsibility and possibility was all-consuming and thrillingly motivating for every employee, no matter how junior or senior their role.

Larry is famous for describing the emotion of passion-driven risk-taking as being "uncomfortably excited." This philosophy has given me guidance in every phase of my career and life since. In my early years at Google, while I was working on the Product team, this translated into helping me navigate the constantly pivoting priorities of the company. We would put our hearts and souls into a product and do our best to execute the perfect launch only to have it canceled later to divert resources and attention to a newer generation of products and ideas. That roller coaster taught me to enjoy the ride—both the ups and the downs.

The key to being recognized for achievements and being seen as someone worthy of advancement and investment within a company is creating a track record of growth. And since growth always comes outside of our comfort zones, I regularly seek out projects that make me stretch beyond my current abilities. This process moves from intolerable to thrilling as long as I am focused on what the end goal means to me.

In my second year at Google, I decided to fully embrace this Google philosophy and make some proposals that were outside my comfort zone but that I felt deeply could increase the effectiveness of our team and help me grow. Marissa ran the Consumer Product team within the larger Product team, and I noticed that because of the pace at which we worked, many of her initiatives within the team were only permeating a level or two down the management chain. The lower levels within our team were not being brought into the process and were inefficiently out of step.

I made the suggestion that while Marissa was leading the weekly management team meeting with her direct reports, I should simultaneously meet with all of the corresponding executive business partners to discuss how these initiatives would affect their teams and how to implement them. It had been a calculated risk to create this responsibility for myself. I had never done anything like that before, so I had to have faith that I was smart enough to figure out how to implement strategy, put together effective agendas, and create something that would save us all time rather than pile another bureaucratic step on top of our already-full workloads.

I was largely ineffective at the beginning, and I had to learn how to earn the respect of my peers and prove to them that I was there to make them more effective and advocate on their behalf rather than there as a judge or spy on behalf of my manager. This took a solid six months of experimenting with different meeting formats, building one-on-one relationships of trust, and learning how to break down team strategies to the individual contributor level. These are the same skills I use today with my consulting clients on a daily basis, decades later.

While the format took months to perfect, hosting these meetings immediately gave me a firsthand account of what was going well and which teams were struggling and in need of guidance or additional resources. This helped me be a much more effective and valuable asset for the Consumer Product team because I was then able to make informed recommendations for how things could be improved. I had purposefully moved myself from a passive role to a proactive one that developed my strategy expertise and gave me opportunities to be seen as a leader and trusted resource.

Lead from Where You Are

This proactive process I'd created allowed a partnership to form between Marissa and me, where she gave direction to the team from the top and I increased the application of her strategy from the bottom up. This measurably increased the efficiency of our team as well as our work-life happiness. I then started to include training exercises in my meeting agendas to meet the needs of the more junior members of the team. This wasn't glamorous, and, in fact, my efforts were largely unnoticed by most senior members of our team. However, I knew that this was an essential element of meeting our team goals, and I was willing to lean into the gritty work needed for the team to be successful.

In general, due to these meetings, we were able to pivot early and often and keep everyone in sync even while our team was growing astronomically and our product-launch cycles were increasing in both number and speed. This also opened up the door for me to take on more project management work that was more demanding, challenging, and critical to the company and helped me grow my skills and role in a way that was really rewarding to me personally.

Once I had proactively taken on the responsibility to help implement my manager's strategy across the team, I became known as the expert in the room for the more-junior members of the team, with whom Marissa had less exposure. This unexpectedly led to me being invited to join the Product team's calibration committee, who evaluated our team members during the evaluation, promotion, and bonus cycles every six months. It was a privilege to be in the room where these decisions were being made by the senior leadership. I was invited there because I had developed a needed expertise and unique perspective, which helped them use their resources more effectively to incentivize and support our growing team.

There are always risks in putting yourself in a new spotlight and open for judgment, criticism, and scrutiny, but there are also risks in staying in your box. I decided that I would rather risk proactively trying to solve a problem and not being successful at my first attempt than being the kind of person who fails the team because of inaction.

The very skill of identifying a need within the team, proactively creating a solution, and enthusiastically attacking without waiting for an invitation is what qualifies you for leadership more than tenure. Bravery and advancement follow a willingness to be uncomfortably excited about your work.

MAKE BIG BETS EARLY

My personal desk at Amazon will likely be in a museum one day. It was an icon when I sat at it back in 2002, and it surely is even more so within the company today.

When Jeff started Amazon in the garage of his rental home in Bellevue, Washington, he eventually tired of kneeling on the hard floor packing boxes to fulfill customer orders. At first, he considered buying knee pads, but then he realized that what he really needed were packing tables. He went shopping for tables at The Home Depot across the street but thought they were unnecessarily expensive for the purpose. Instead, he bought plain wood doors that were on sale and crafted his own tables for packing orders for shipment. My desk at Amazon was one of the three original door-desks made by Jeff's own hands in that start-up garage a few years earlier. It was a physical reminder of the grittiness, sacrifice, and humility necessary to make his dream a reality.

These door-desks became a symbol of the core company value of frugality, which is one of Amazon's official fourteen leadership principles. In fact, Jeff rewards the most innovative ideas presented by a company employee at the annual all-hands meeting by presenting them with a miniature replica, the Door Desk Award.

Allocating Limited Resources

Even more motivating for me than the Door Desk Award, perhaps slightly influenced by the fact that I sat at the original version every single day, was the Just Do It Award. I never won it, but I can certainly say that I tried! The Just Do It Award was named after Nike's well-known slogan and was given to someone who put the company's fourteen leadership principles into effect without slowing down to ask for permission. They just simply did the right thing.

While I was at Amazon, the Just Do It Award was once given to a woman working in one of our fulfillment centers. While she was packing boxes, she noticed the glaring fluorescent glow coming from the fleet of vending machines in the breakrooms. She thought that they were unnecessarily wasting energy, so she just reached inside and turned half of the bulbs off. This ended up saving a significant enough amount in Amazon's energy costs that it later got noticed by management.

I tried to follow this example and embody the company values as much as I could, even as an extremely junior member of the company. I remember that when Amazon was launching the beauty category on the website, we wanted to do it as frugally as possible. Rather than hiring a traditional agency or paying professional models, we decided that it would be more reflective of our values to have our employees be the models. I helped the beauty launch team recruit and assemble as diverse a range of employees as possible to be the face of the launch. I was thrilled when the girl who worked part-time in our office opening mail was selected to be a core face of the launch. This was not only the most frugal choice for the company, but it also put the diversity of our customers front and center.

I feel fortunate to have experienced Amazon at a time when it was scrappy and the company's survival depended on each and every employee's determination to be creative and agile. Amazon has remained dominant decades later because of Jeff Bezos's famous Day One mindset, which permeates every layer of the company: he treats each day like it is the first day of the company, where success is not guaranteed.

Today, we tend to think that Amazon's success was inevitable. How could it not be? At the time, though, that was not true at all. During those early years, the run-up to Amazon's initial public offering and the period after were met with frequent skepticism, critical headlines, and occasionally outright mockery. Jeff often said that "entrepreneurs must be willing to be misunderstood for long periods of time." Many do not have the stomach for that and give up too early or don't try at all.

Jeff reminds himself of this daily, not only by sitting at his *own* handmade door-desk, but also by naming his new Seattle office building Day 1.

While our individual goals might not be realized by becoming one of the wealthiest people in the world like Jeff, we can follow his behavior patterns for unprecedented success within our own right.

Be an Active Learner

While Jeff's results are unparalleled, the opportunities to apply these leadership lessons to "normal" lives and goals are limitless. I have to allow myself to take the time necessary to discover what passion project drives me so much that I'm willing to make big bets and consistently live outside my comfort zone.

I have never met a truly impactful person who didn't first learn to appreciate the way in which the smaller tasks become the catalyst to unprecedented results. You have to be humble enough to be down on your knees, if necessary, to make your dreams come to life. Many people are lured by mediocre achievements available within their comfort zones and rob themselves of the thrill and joy of knowing that they found their limits and pushed past them.

My personal experience with learning to apply the lessons of great leadership to my own start-up was a bigger challenge that I had expected after decades of apprenticeship. When I got brave enough to leave my career in Silicon Valley and stake a claim of my own, I definitely was not an instant success. Far from it! The first few years I felt the dreaded fear of wondering not only if I was going to survive it, but, even worse, if I was quickly losing relevance in the industry. I felt small and invisible without the big names of Google or Amazon at my side. Rather than giving in to that nearly crippling fear, I decided to double down and apply the lessons I had learned throughout my career anew. I needed to switch gears from being reactive and small to becoming an active learner and to unapologetically growing alongside my ambitions.

I quickly realized that in order to become the essential advisor my consulting-client CEOs needed, I would have to return to my habit of industry homework and hone my approach and expertise. I needed to treat my job like my own personal business school yet again.

I started prioritizing spending the first half of the day reading as many books and articles as I could about the themes I was discussing with my clients. I found myself, again, researching every name I didn't recognize and every term I didn't understand for the industries I was now serving. I devoured academic journals, case studies, and texts that challenged my thinking and introduced me to business practices and models I had no personal experience with.

If I hoped to translate my Silicon Valley experiences and best practices into the diverse industries of my clients, I would need to actively research and experiment with them to see which translated and which did not apply. I had to become an expert not only in corporate strategy but also in fields as diverse as FinTech, AgTech, artificial intelligence, and everything in between. I could not do so in theory, hiding behind a book or my fear of making a mistake. I had to experiment, pivot, and put my learning into practice before I was sure of the final results.

Becoming an active learner rather than a passive worker can turn nearly any job into a milestone—upon which you can build astronomical success—but it is also terrifying at times because you are living at the edge of your understanding and honed instincts. This was the only way I could qualify myself for the consulting work I'd been hired to do, and it was also my only chance to grow at the pace I knew my clients would need me to in order to continue to contribute and help drive results. Once again I had to remember that I needed to consider massive continued learning to be part of my job description and not a disqualifier for it. I had to learn to be passionate, gritty, unafraid of failure, and uncomplacent just as Jeff, Marissa, and Eric had taught me to be.

Life is an eternal school, and you are in charge of the curriculum.

CHAPTER 7 ROI SPRINT

Do you long for something different or bigger for your life? Are you willing to make sacrifices to realize your goals? The true secret is that this method doesn't require you to work harder or longer. It ensures that you are taking the right risks and using your energy and resources efficiently to propel yourself powerfully forward. What is your particular work-life rhythm that balances your passions, values, and work?

The essential element in achieving impactful goals is giving up the comfort of the status quo for the hope of creating something revolutionary, which by definition is unfamiliar and challenging.

Is there a way for you to use your limited resources or junior status to your advantage? Do you have a unique observation or access to a part of your team that you can turn into an opportunity for project leadership? Is there a peer who is one or two steps ahead of you to whom you can look for inspiration or an example of the growth path you want to follow? Have you given yourself stretch projects and time for creative thinking? What are the ways in which you can turn your learning into action today?

Recognize: What aspiration do you have that makes you uncomfortably excited? What is your team currently struggling with that you could try to resolve? What can you volunteer to do today that you're uniquely able to offer?

Own: What do you need to learn or practice to move yourself closer to this big-bet goal? What rhythm do you need in order to ensure your long-term effectiveness?

Implement: Put a big bet in motion today!

PIVOT POINTS
AND REINVENTION

*P*ivots are part of every life and career—whether intentional or not. Having a strategy in place before these moments of disruption arrive gives you a competitive advantage and preemptively reduces some of the inevitable stress. Some of the pivots in my life have been wonderfully empowering, and some were simply gut-wrenching, but each taught me valuable lessons that I doubt I could have learned any other way.

The hardest pivots are those that come from a sudden loss of something you hold most dear and consider part of your very self-definition. Even chosen, purposeful pivots can often bring up the same feelings of stress because they require us to let go of something good with the faith that it will be replaced by something great, which is a process that can test our faith and resolve.

Pivots can either break us down or build us up. Many do both. There are strategies for managing the pressures of these life changes so that we come out the other side better off than we had been before. Doing the following things will help with your next pivot:

- Learning to manage the pressures of growth
- Claiming your power
- Finding and following the right Sherpa

When I look back at my career, I see a growth pattern that wasn't obvious to me in the moment. As Steve Jobs explained in his commencement address at Stanford University, the dots that make up the course of our life often only connect and make sense in retrospect. This is part of what can be so disorienting during moments of pivot.

This has certainly been true for me, and perhaps that resonates with you too. I didn't come into the workforce at twenty years old with a master plan for how to get to work side by side with the most powerful people in the world. But I did enter with an insatiable drive to learn and an unquenched ambition deep inside, and I stayed committed to learning as much as possible in the process. At a minimum those dots were within my power to connect regardless of the unexpected path I took to do so.

I wish that I could have had a coach to help me bring a personal plan into focus much earlier, but I am grateful for the life-changing experiences that came my way and the wisdom I was exposed to daily. I am glad I eventually found ways to take charge during seasons of change and was able to feel a semblance of control in the process.

LEARNING TO MANAGE
THE PRESSURES OF GROWTH

While at Amazon in the early 2000s, I watched Jeff Bezos build pivots into the culture and core fiber of the company from day one. Very few companies have this wisdom and foresight early on, and this is often the differentiator between those that scale and dominate and those that fail to convert. Jeff did not wait until the company outgrew its current systems and pipelines before he invested in and invented new ones. He knew that in order to fulfill his vision of building one of the most impactful companies in the world, he would need to pivot constantly. He set up pivots as a system indicator of success, which means that change is celebrated rather than feared in the Amazon culture.

Jeff refers to this pivot culture as the Day One mindset. In a Day One mindset, companies adapt to emerging technologies, trends, and market demands and build critical pivots into their business models. These organizations are quick to pivot with fast-paced decision-making and have a flat management structure to remove any barriers that might keep innovative ideas from being heard and adopted. The dreaded Day Two scenarios happen when companies grow large and become encumbered by bureaucracy, rigidity, and complacent risk aversion.

Jeff designed Amazon to be both nimble and robust. This is the right model for individual careers as well.

Avoiding Complacency

Jeff explained Amazon's growth strategy to me as one that does not tolerate entropy. Entropy, a term Jeff borrowed from thermodynamics, is a measure of unavailable energy in a closed system and a measure of a system's disorder. Without an active plan to combat it, Jeff saw inefficiencies inevitably creep in as companies grow, making them rigid and unresponsive to change.

Entropy happens in individuals as well. There are times when we get complacent and continue following patterns and habits that no longer correspond to our values or drive us toward larger goals. The comforts of habit and familiarity mask this wasted potential as the wiser or at least safer choice. The growth and greater happiness that comes when we are maximizing our talents and resources and consistently stretching toward something new can feel threatening and even disorienting at first.

The irony is that when we make these conscious efforts to make purposeful change, we are in more control than we were while resting in our comfort zones, where the responsibility for our future is delegated to another. We are less likely to become victims of unanticipated life change when we ourselves are the change agents and are in charge of its implementation.

Life throws all of us unexpected trials, tests, and heartaches. What we do with these moments is the great differentiator in our fates. Sometimes these come as a surprise, and sometimes they are challenges of our own choosing. It is essential that we learn through these experiences which discomforts we should lean into to reap the richest rewards and which pains are telling us to make a change and choose another path. Building this wisdom can be very taxing because it comes through the exhaustion of trial and error.

You have to be sure of your ultimate goals in order to not get lost in the twists and turns of pivots. Just like a professional ballerina traveling across the stage in a series of pirouettes, you need to be able to spot and keep your eye firmly on a single point so that you do not get dizzy and fall off course as you go.

Even the most powerful CEOs in the world experience moments of self-doubt. The difference between high performers and those who concede their power to someone else is not the lack of fear or even imposter syndrome. The difference lies in how long we allow ourselves to live in that headspace.

Moments of Doubt

In June of 2017, I was with Eric Schmidt in Paris for the Viva Technology conference when he taught me an important aspect of always pushing yourself forward and not being held back by a past definition of self. We had just created a speech with his speechwriter, Matt, about the new age of abundance the world was entering with the dawn of machine learning and artificial intelligence. It was a hopeful speech meant to ease concerns over the fast-moving pace of technological advancement and assure the global audience that these technologies could be harnessed for the greater good and provide new job and advancement opportunities for all levels and types of industry.

Eric is a gifted speaker and highly experienced, but he seemed a little nervous before going onstage, which was unusual. This was likely because the speech was brand new and because he was going to be followed by Emmanuel Macron, the newly elected president of France, whose speech was about his goal of making France "the nation for start-ups."

Before taking the stage, Eric and I split away from the inevitable entourage of staffers so Eric could focus on his message and the flow of this newly drafted speech. Eric and I were both drenched in sweat because there was no air movement backstage at the conference center and it was a very hot day in Paris. The security team with President Macron had taped the doors shut with a safety seal after they cleared each room prior to his arrival, so there wasn't even the faintest hope of a draft. Sweat was dripping down my back as Eric took the stage.

One of Eric's greatest gifts is being able to explain highly complex technologies in a way that makes them understandable to even the least tech-savvy person. This speech about artificial intelligence was the start of the wave of AI being discussed over watercoolers and dinner tables rather than just in elite research universities. Eric takes this role as a statesman of technology very seriously, and he always pushes himself to do better, to reach more people, and to be of more assistance to the global community. He seeks out this pressure, but he also still feels it.

When Eric got offstage after his speech, I knew that he would come to me for notes and feedback as he always did. However, I put my notebook of feedback down when he walked directly toward me and asked, earnestly yet softly, "Was that okay?" I laughed a little, completely taken aback, and said, "Of course that was okay! You are Eric Schmidt!" He just shook his head with a smile and said, "You know, sometimes I still have to remind myself that I'm not little Eric from Virginia anymore."

I have been surrounded by celebrities, heads of state, CEOs, and every kind of power you can imagine for the last two decades. I am here to tell you that they all, without exception, experience moments of imposter syndrome, doubts, and discouragement. We all experience these moments, and we all need occasional reminders that we deserve to be center stage in our own life and firmly in the spotlight. The differentiator here is that high performers experience this as an imposter moment rather than a syndrome. They do not let this moment define them as a permanent diagnosis or state of being.

Eric's moment of humility, and his willingness to share that with me, gave me permission to realize then and there that I am no longer little Ann from Seattle anymore. I, too, deserve to claim my seat at any table that I've earned the right to through relentless training, work, and my own battle scars.

CLAIMING YOUR POWER

The year 2016 was one of dramatic change for me both professionally and personally in ways I had not anticipated. This upcoming major pivot point in my life started out small soon after the death of a colleague in 2015.

For years my team and I spent one day a week working from the Google X campus, where Eric chaired the weekly senior-management meeting. We sat in this factory of moonshot ideas surrounded by the best and the brightest dreamers I have ever encountered. I witnessed them take seemingly impossible ideas from conception to launch over the course of a decade, led by Sergey Brin, Google's cofounder, and Astro Teller. I watched them invent the technologies necessary to make driverless cars a reality in Waymo and build high-altitude balloons that can rise up to the stratosphere to create an aerial wireless network of 4G internet to serve rural communities in Project Loon. One of these engineers was a brilliant guy named Dan Fredinburg.

Dan and I weren't friends socially, but we started at Google just six months apart and saw each other and exchanged pleasantries at least once a week for nine years. Dan was the kind of guy who lived life to the absolute fullest. He worked as the head of privacy at Google X and also founded the Google Adventure team, which set out to map remote locations, such as the Great Barrier Reef and mountain ranges, with Google Earth–quality photos so that people could experience these wonders even if they were not able to travel there themselves. He was motivated to help people experience, appreciate, and strive to protect the natural beauty of our planet.

Tragically, Dan was one of four Google employees documenting Mount Everest ascent routes when he was killed in an avalanche caused by an earthquake while doing what he loved most. He was thirty-three years old.

Living Fearlessly

After Dan's death, his family set up a charity in his honor and started a website called Live Dan, where they encouraged those who were inspired by him to "pledge to live life fearlessly," just as Dan had. Reading that statement woke me up because, at the time, I was in a very difficult period of my personal life.

Despite years of therapy, tearful conversations, and my outright protest, my fifteen-year marriage was coming to an end that year. The story of my divorce doesn't feel like mine to tell because it was the decision of my ex-husband for reasons that belong to him alone. What I can say is that I didn't deal with it well.

I spent several years in the denial phase of my grief. I dealt with that trauma by working out excessively and spending unreasonably long hours in the office to avoid my personal misery of being alone. It struck me then that if I passed away, I absolutely would not have wanted anyone to try and *live like Ann*. That was a sobering moment.

Dan's family wrote the following challenge: "Living Dan is living life as you are, who you are, and who you want to be. Nothing is unachievable. Sometimes that means taking the more difficult, less traveled roads; Dan . . . took the untraveled roads. He was the ruler of his own life's journey. [He explored] a limitless world of possibility and happiness." I wanted to not only embody that but to become an inspiration to empower others to do so as well. This has taken on many forms over the years.

They say that a crisis is a horrible thing to waste, and I can tell you that once I accepted my fate, I ran with this new reality of unlimited possibilities to the extremes. I decided to become the author of my own destiny. I decided that rather than wallow in mourning what I had lost, I had better put all that energy into creating something I could be proud of. I wanted this new phase of my life to be synonymous with excitement, bravery, and achievements.

I started to seek out adventures. I discovered a renewed joy in doing hard things. Notice that I didn't say in *accomplishing* hard things. Actual joy lives in the attempt and not just the summit of our personal mountains. When we only focus on that last, singular moment at the end of the journey, we miss the milestones that deserve celebration: strength gained, knowledge earned, and fears conquered. The journey is the only part fully within our individual control. The result is most often out of our hands. We can't control how our work is received. We can only control being brave enough to try, and once we find joy in that pursuit, our lives become richer and true happiness is attainable.

My first steps toward this new life philosophy were small and measured. I simply started to say yes to things I normally would have said no to, and unforeseen doors started opening.

Stepping Onto the Stage

Out of the blue I was approached by someone I had never met who had just seen my profile on LinkedIn, and this person invited me to speak at a conference in New York just a few months away. I had never given a speech before, nor even attended a conference aimed at the chief-of-staff role before, so my first gut reaction was to say no. But when I looked at my calendar, I saw that I was going to be working from the New York office that week anyway, and something inside of me felt like it might be worth a try. The truth was that I didn't know a single person who would be attending, so even if it was a huge failure, there wouldn't be any real harm done. At a minimum, I figured it was an opportunity to learn.

I went to that conference not knowing what to expect. I was the only speaker who presented without a PowerPoint presentation. I just had some notes and stories jotted down to share, and I spoke from my heart about things I have learned, often the hard way, in my career. I was a complete novice on a roster of professional speakers, but I didn't want my imperfect presentation to hold me back from sharing things I thought could be of value to others.

I was naturally nervous before I stepped onto the stage. Thankfully, once I started to talk, my nerves disappeared, and I was relaxed enough to speak authentically and connect with the audience.

To my great relief, the feedback afterward was positive, and I enjoyed talking to the attendees about the parts of my story that resonated with them. I am sure I would be embarrassed to watch a playback of my speech today, but I am unquestionably glad that I took a risk because of the doors that have opened to me since.

Immediately after my speech, one of the conference speakers, Vickie, came up to me to congratulate me on my first talk and asked if I would like some feedback on my presentation. I had watched her present a technical training on Microsoft products, and I'd loved her entire presentation and was drawn in during the full two hours even though I didn't ever use any Microsoft products myself and didn't need the training specifically. She was an engaging speaker and cleverly balanced her deep technical expertise with her quick sense of humor to keep the audience engaged.

I was so touched that she would offer me feedback and help me develop this new skill. We exchanged contact information, and she called me a week later, a few days before Thanksgiving, to talk through specific tips she had that would make my presentation better organized and easier for the audience to remember in the long term. She thought that the raw content of my talk was impactful and unique and that I was a natural presenter. She really encouraged me to keep speaking.

Vickie is a rare example of someone in my career who noticed a raw talent of mine and proactively took the time to coach me on how to do it better. She followed through with some easy-to-apply advice that improved my talk instantly—she encouraged me to organize it into five easy-to-remember principles illustrated by the stories of my career. I would have been far too intimidated back then to have asked her for this advice myself.

I have since spoken on stages on five different continents and have met lifelong friends at these events who have quite literally changed my life. And all because I said yes to an invitation to speak before I felt like I was ready to be any good at it. I get so much satisfaction sharing my experiences with like-minded, ambitious people trying to level-up and make the most of their career opportunities.

I also used this new skill to help Google by speaking at global training events in our Dublin and New York offices about how employees can grow their careers and influence. It felt rewarding to pass on so many of the lessons I had learned to those coming up in the company after me.

I had a pinch-me moment when, two years later, I was invited to speak at SXSW in Austin, Texas, for the first time on the day before Eric Schmidt himself was speaking. We flew to the conference together on his jet. While the sizes of our assigned stages at the conference were noticeably different, it was a wonderful moment for me as his self-appointed apprentice to share that experience.

Failure in the Spotlight

This is not to say that I haven't had massive failures in this same arena. I was once invited to speak at an enormous conference in Milwaukee very early in my speaking-career days for an audience that was very different from my usual crowd of innovators and disrupters. They put me on their largest stage in front of thousands of people. I was thrilled at the opportunity to connect and share with such a large audience. However, I could sense right away that neither I nor my material really resonated in the usual way. Very few of them even bothered to talk to me after I came offstage.

After I returned to California, I asked the organizers to send me feedback so that I could improve my presentation and delivery skills. I knew that it hadn't been a smash success, so I was expecting some big areas where I could improve. Per my request, they gave me unfiltered access to the attendee feedback on my session, and it was brutal. I easily could have cried and never, ever stepped on a stage again. It was momentarily humiliating. The feedback was the opposite to my experience with Vickie years before, when she offered suggestions that made me and the delivery of my message better. By contrast, there wasn't anything in the Milwaukee attendee feedback that was concrete or actionable. They simply didn't relate to or like me.

While it absolutely hurt my ego temporarily, I came to realize something essential: that it simply wasn't my audience. I'm not for everyone, and I don't need to be. I have never had a more liberating realization in all my life. If I hadn't embraced that fact, I never would have spoken on stages closer aligned to my ideal audience, like entrepreneurs at SXSW.

Power in Letting Go

In the process of my personal reinvention, I realized that California might no longer be my correct stage either. There was too much of my old life and my former self represented there.

Over the course of the first three months of 2017, I sold or donated nearly everything I owned: my car, house, furniture, clothes, art, you name it. I had to touch and mourn every single belonging I had collected during my marriage and watch it walk out the front door—every wedding gift, every memory, every dream. It was agonizing, and I cried myself to sleep more nights than not. When the last thing was walked out the door, I had only two suitcases and three duffle bags remaining to my name. The process had been excruciating, but the moment it was complete, I immediately felt the sense of relief I had been chasing. And this was just the beginning of the radical changes I was making in my life.

My job at Google was my safety net and was my only remaining sense of personal identity and source of pride. But I knew that I needed to risk some part of that in order to start the next chapter.

I pitched Eric on the idea of me transferring to the London office for a few months. The United Kingdom had just voted in support of the Brexit referendum to leave the European Union six months earlier. No one knew what that was going to mean for European businesses and the economy. Just a few months later, the French and German presidential elections were scheduled, and we expected even more turnover in the political and business landscape.

I suggested to Eric that it might be helpful for me to sit with our European policy and communications teams and to drive our team efforts of the executive chairman from there so that we could stay proactive on these important developments and relationships. There was a clear business case for me to develop and deepen strategic political relationships in Europe and to leverage our influence and expertise to meet the company goals. To my relief, Eric agreed.

I closed the door to my house in Sunnyvale, California, for the last time on April 1, 2017, and I moved to London without a clear plan for what would happen next. For the first time in my life, I was anchorless and free of any attachments or expectations. Given my usual careful personality and temperament, this was my ultimate expression of a full midlife crisis, and I was determined to bridle it.

I was able to fully uproot my life and live with generous friends in cities around the world for the next two years as a nomad. I was free to reinvent myself in every imaginable way without limitations. I was halfway across the tightrope, and there was no advantage to going backward rather than forward. Limited options can bring out boldness and clarity that you might not dare to tap into otherwise. I decided that I didn't want to have to keep proving my worthiness, to myself or anyone else, anymore. I simply wanted to love my life for all that it is.

Google remained my parachute as I jumped off that cliff of self-discovery. I found a new home and belonging among my colleagues in London. We worked very hard and collaborated on projects that felt important and impactful globally, which gave me a renewed sense of identity and purpose. I felt like I was at the center of some small part of the global history that took place that summer.

I collaborated with the London-based team on the Google Camp conference, which brings together the most powerful people in the world for a week in Italy to tackle global issues. I also worked with the communications, events, and policy teams to coordinate the Google Zeitgeist, where Eric interviewed Queen Rania of Jordan as well as Tony Blair onstage. I also collaborated with the Google Cultural Institute team to do a launch event at the Natural History Museum, where they had digitized the entire collection to make it accessible to anyone in the world for free. In Germany I arranged strategic meetings with Angela Merkel, the newly reelected chancellor of Germany, about how to design government policies to incentivize and support local entrepreneurship. We also attended the Munich Security Conference to connect with military decision makers, about developing technologies such as artificial intelligence, and with strategic industry partners like BMW, to discuss the future of driverless cars.

I was building a new rudder for my life, but I hadn't yet found my North Star. I needed a guide.

Finding and Following the Right Sherpa

Silicon Valley has a deep tradition of formal mentors for the highest levels of tech talent. This dovetails with the culture of continued learning and exploration. Even after Eric Schmidt had spent ten years as Google's CEO and then settled into a good rhythm of what he wanted to contribute as the executive chairman of Alphabet, he still continued making concentrated efforts to grow and be inspired to new heights. A big part of this involved seeking out mentors.

Just like Olympic athletes, Eric understood that while he was one of the best in the world at what he did, he needed continual coaching and a neutral, external observer to bring out the best in him. Eric's longtime mentor was Bill Campbell. Bill was the mentor to the Silicon Valley elite and brought with him a wealth of experience. For fifteen years Bill coached executives at Google, Intuit, eBay, Yahoo!, Twitter, and Facebook.

The most impressive thing to me about Bill wasn't his collection of A-list CEO clients; it was the way he treated everyone like they were the most important person in the world to him. His kindness was unmistakable. He could have easily walked right past me with just a smile, but instead he spent time making me feel like a valuable part of the team and like someone he cared about.

When Bill died of cancer in 2016 at the age of seventy-five, Apple delayed their quarterly earnings call, for the first time in history, in order to host his memorial personally. I sat in that memorial with some of the most powerful executives in the world and cried with them while we shared hilarious stories about Bill and the lessons he had taught us.

Bill's mentorship style can be summarized as a whole-person approach. He never focused on a specific business challenge without incorporating the larger picture and helping the executives he was advising to remember who they are, what they valued, and what they wanted to contribute to the world. The pain that comes with losing a loved one is often accompanied by the gift of reexamining your life to be sure you are on track and focusing your energy on what truly matters to you.

Creating Your Mentor Avatar

I was lucky to have access to some of the greatest minds in the world, and I wanted to be more thoughtful about how I could use that to inspire my vision for an even higher level of contribution. I decided that if I was going to have the personal growth I longed for, I needed to build up my own network of support.

The truth is that you don't need access to a billionaire's Rolodex to have that same level of inspiration and coaching that opens doors for you. In fact, some people whom I consider my long-term mentors don't even know I exist because our only interaction is me following them online. I've created a composite mentor from watching many people whose skills and careers I admire, and I put a little piece of each of them into my inspirational role model avatar.

In order to determine who was best to guide me, I had to know where I was trying to go. I sat down and wrote my dream résumé, full of the things I wanted to learn and accomplish as I progressed in my career. I have found that being learning-focused rather than title-focused has allowed me to identify opportunities for massive impact that I might have missed otherwise.

One of my greatest fears has been living a life of insignificance. I am terrified of that fate enough to make the risk-taking necessary in becoming exceptional worth the inevitable missteps, embarrassments, and judgments of people not on a similar path.

One of the most important steps has been to establish not only what I want to do with my limited days on earth, but why I want to do it and with whom.

The first step of creating my dream future résumé was looking for people who were five or ten years ahead of me in accomplishing my big goals. I knew I wanted to be a founder, so I looked for those who embodied the characteristics I wanted to emulate in my leadership and actively studied their paths, pivots, and best practices. I knew I wanted to speak on global stages, so I researched who was currently speaking to my dream audience and learned everything I could about the long path that qualified them to be on those stages. I knew I wanted to focus my work on empowering and educating entrepreneurs to live lives of fulfillment and meaning, so I sought out leaders who were engaged in social good and studied how they got their voices heard. I have interviewed as many as have been willing to talk to me and done my research on those I've yet to meet.

This search for the right mentors is an ongoing quest for me. What I have absolutely learned is that no one of lasting impact became a success overnight. That means that I have had to design a strategy that I can sustain even in the early periods of obscurity. That is a lonely path if you feel like you're walking it alone, so I try to find out as much as I can about the pathway to success I've seen in others and then reverse engineer a way to get to where they are now. When I find thought leaders I admire, I like to see where they first got their start, who is in their professional network, and what conferences they attend, and then I look for ways I can emulate this progression.

You don't need an elite personal network to learn from the very best in the age of the internet!

Don't Stop for Permission

I came to realize that, from day one, I had treated my jobs like an apprenticeship and gleaned as much learning as possible from each day, so mentorship had been built into my daily experience. I felt I fully came into my own once I started sharing that experience with like-minded people around me. That is why I enjoyed speaking at conferences and coaching and cheering on other ambitious people. It's satisfying to try and pay that forward as much as I can now, and I've realized that I learn at a completely different level when I'm teaching and mentoring myself.

I have seen so many lackluster people become leaders across the globe simply because they were boldly confident and raised their hands long before they knew what they were doing. Anyone wanting to be seen as a leader needs to shift their focus from contributing to driving. Eric often says that the biggest difference between a true leader and a manager is that leaders inspire and managers tell people what to do. It is as simple as that. At some point in your career, stepping into the spotlight becomes your job, and it's entirely up to you to claim your place on the stage boldly.

I left Google on September 1, 2018, after twelve years in my dream job at the company rated number one to work for in America, and I started anew and alone. On the surface that sounds crazy, and I still have moments when I question this decision. Google had been my home, my extended family, my identity, and my comfort zone for over a decade. And now, for the first time in my professional life, I am building a dream of my own rather than being paid to build someone else's.

In my post-Google life, I have built myself up again from scratch in so many important ways—in a new country, speaking a new language, immersed in a new culture, and cultivating a new network. Those kinds of risks can be terrifying. But what has held me together when I felt like it was all too much are those principles of success that I learned from my work in Silicon Valley and the mentors who have helped me find my North Star. What I want most in life and my career is to contribute value that empowers others to create the good we want to see in the world. Knowing where my values and passions lie makes the disorienting, scary, and exhausting process of entrepreneurship possible to navigate.

I reverted back to the practice of out-caring everyone around me, rather than trying to outwork them. I offer things to my work and clients that go beyond the projects, problems, or challenges I've been asked to solve. I prioritize the quality and insightfulness of my work rather than just the hours contributed to it or the end result. With this mindset, I look deeper into what my clients are really trying to solve, create, and contribute, and I get immediately to the heart of that. I have found deep personal growth through mentoring others along their journeys.

I have been relieved to find that this cycle of learning to manage the pressures of growth, claiming my power through doing hard things, and finding and not only following the right Sherpa but becoming one myself has led me to discover that the ability to claim my future has been inside of me all along.

I no longer feel the need to say someone else's name before my own in order to qualify for a seat at the table. In reality, these many pivots, however long or painful, have given me the tools I needed not to reinvent myself, but rather to unveil who I really was all along.

I have realized that I am enough.

CHAPTER 8 ROI SPRINT

Have you let complacency rob you of the adventures that life is ready and waiting to give you? Are you able to forge through moments of doubt and remind yourself of how far you have already come? In what ways can you claim your power today and live fearlessly? What stage do you want to be on and to be known for? Are you ready to let go of whatever is holding you back? What mentor avatar can you create and emulate today in order to take one bold step closer to where and who you want to be?

Recognize: Has entropy crept into your daily habits? Could you invite more joy into your work by taking on a new challenge? Are you living a life that you recommend others emulate? Do you have mentors who inspire your next steps? Have you taken the time to craft your own dream future résumé?

Own: What growth project can you take on to move you closer to advancement? Are you surrounded by people who will sponsor your growth and move you in the direction you want to go?

Implement: Ask for something this week that will move you closer to your ideals in your work.

KNOW YOUR VALUE

Resilience, it turns out, isn't a skill you learn once and are done. It is like a muscle that you need to flex and fatigue on a regular basis in order for it to remain strong. My transition into being an entrepreneur and founding my own company is the most extreme daily exercise I've experienced so far in my career. This is how you discover what you understand only in theory and what you know how to do in actual practice.

Discovering my actual value has centered around building a core confidence that lives inside of me and is independent of any title, company, or external sponsorship. I hunt for my value daily, but I have found three key ways to bring it out. You can, too, by doing the following:

- Repackage your skills.
- Create a personal business plan.
- Remember that strength follows the struggle.

Despite my entrepreneur education from elite mentors, I have found this process to be equal parts exhausting and thrilling. It all started out innocently enough.

REPACKAGE YOUR SKILLS

As I started to share with colleagues that I was planning to leave Google after twelve years at the company, some of them reached out to me with opportunities that I wouldn't have even dared apply for normally, which was very encouraging.

Over the last decade of working with Eric Schmidt, I had often worked on projects with his venture capital firm, Innovation Endeavors. They have a special, values-driven approach to investments, which attracts the kind of entrepreneurs I relate to the most. Dror Berman, the CEO of Innovation Endeavors, would occasionally introduce me to one of their promising portfolio CEOs and ask me to help walk them through a specific growth problem they were having.

Over the years, I had met many of these young start-up CEOs and loved answering some of their operations and procedural questions about running their companies. It came naturally to me to share with them some of my best practices and things I had learned from Jeff Bezos, Marissa Mayer, and Eric Schmidt across my career. I loved these coffee chats and found it fascinating and inspiring to help them through some of their early decision points.

While I was working full-time, it was hard to engage with them very systematically because my time was limited and I had unpredictable availability. I also didn't have any formal methodology training for this kind of business mentoring, so it was hard to know where to begin. I don't know how helpful I ever really was in those early conversations, but I know for a fact that I learned a lot from the process.

Once I made the final decision to leave Google, a few of these CEOs asked if they could make our mentor relationship formal. I thought it would be fun to work on some projects and keep my Silicon Valley connections strong while doing some soul searching in Europe. I had decided to move to Spain, a true polar opposite location from Silicon Valley, so I could truly reinvent myself from the ground up. Unintentionally, that was the first stage of forming my company, where I now specialize in C-suite optimization, leadership strategies, and reverse engineering moonshot goals. It has evolved a lot over the last few years, but that foundation was the next opportunity I hadn't realized I was cultivating all along while at Google.

Jumping into the Unknown

I started off with what I thought would be baby steps into consulting with familiar faces. My first client was a CEO whom I had known for a long time. He is a brilliant, heartfelt, mission-driven CEO and exactly the kind of leader I felt comfortable working with. This company was an agriculture tech start-up building indoor farms that use 99 percent less land and 95 percent less water than traditional farming to grow pesticide-free and non-GMO crops, which are healthier for plants, people, and the planet. They are committed to providing fresh produce in underserved markets that is also more nutritionally robust than possible with traditional farming. I felt strongly about their mission, so it felt like a great place to devote some time.

My first collaboration with the CEO was to help the company better coordinate among teams and senior leadership in remote locations across multiple states. They were growing fast and needed systems that would scale. This was a fun challenge, and I felt confident in my expertise in this space.

Then they asked me to help them with a project in the Middle East. Dubai was offering incentives to start-up companies to set up offices in the UAE with the hope of creating a Silicon Valley of the Middle East. The company was interested in exploring these incentives and asked if I would go to Dubai to help move the negotiations forward.

The UAE desperately needed agricultural advances because food was a national security issue, since they could not rely on friendly neighboring countries to always meet the needs of their citizens. Peacetime relationships cannot be taken for granted, so a solution like indoor farming could be a win for everyone. While I had never negotiated electricity rates with government officials before, I did know the chief operating officer for the Dubai Future Foundation who could open some doors for me. He was the former advisor on futures, foresight, and innovation in the UAE prime minister's office. So I got on a plane and set off to try and do something I had never done before, feeling both terrified and excited.

I talked to my sister, who worked with me at Google for most of my time there, before I flew to Dubai. I told her that I was being sent there to negotiate with the local government on electricity rates, which were critical to deciding if this could be a profitable business expansion for the company I was working with. She rightfully asked me, "You do that? You know how to do that?" I answered firmly, "No, I have no idea how to do that. But I think I'll figure it out along the way!" There was no other way!

The trip started off with nervous energy only about my talking points, since all of the lingo around agricultural technology, or AgTech, was new to me. But I studied my notes and memorized my talking points on the very long flights from Spain to Dubai. Unfortunately, my talking points soon became the very least of my worries.

I came down with the absolute worst flu of my life while traveling. I had a stabbing sinus headache, a cough, and a fever. I bought every medication I could carry in the airport pharmacy upon arrival in Dubai before collapsing into a cab. By the time I arrived at the Fairmont Dubai Hotel, I was visibly so ill that they sent me immediately to my room without the usual, formal check-in procedures, and the hotel manager proactively sent up tea to my room. I collapsed into bed but wasn't able to sleep a wink despite having flown all day and arriving at the hotel just after two o'clock in the morning local time.

The next morning I could barely move myself from the bed to the shower, but I was determined to put on my best performance in front of very intimidating government officials.

I was the only woman in the meeting room who was not there to serve tea. As long as I kept my answers very short, I could get through a sentence without coughing. And I kept the tea servers very busy refilling my cup with hot water, lemon, and honey to stifle my cough. Miraculously, I made it through the meeting, which became the first of many great conversations we would have over the next six months.

Even though the Dubai project didn't ultimately proceed, it was a testament to myself that I was capable of running high-stakes meetings, when in the past I would have just been writing the briefing documents for someone else to present. My confidence grew, and I suddenly saw a new vision for what I was personally capable of doing.

My flu symptoms only worsened while I was in Dubai, but I could not go home yet. I had agreed to speak at a launch event in London for my newest client, who was the CEO of a travel-app start-up. We had been introduced through a mutual friend, and it seemed like the ideal partnership for me to consult with her. I was very excited to work with a female founder, and her company was aimed at executive travelers. I felt like I could easily help guide her as she got her company off the ground. Unfortunately, I did not deliver my A game for her.

On the flight from Dubai to London, my eardrums nearly burst from the pressure of takeoff and landing. I literally cried from the pain, and the flight attendants even asked me if I needed an emergency landing. I stupidly pushed through the pain and was sure I would be better off once I got to London. I went to the launch event looking like I had the plague and could not get through my speech without coughing. I did my best to do the taped media interviews, meet with the attendees, and bond with the team, whom I was meeting face-to-face for the first time. I was upset that I couldn't deliver more.

More than not delivering the kind of speech worthy of her launch event, I found myself so overwhelmed with starting my company that I wasn't delivering my usual consistent, proactive help to her. I was scattered, overwhelmed, and ineffective. It was miserable because I knew I was capable of much more, but I struggled to know how to bring that out in this new environment, where I was in charge of everything—accounting, contracts, briefings, travel planning, speechwriting, and more. I was failing not only my client but also myself.

Trusting Your Gut

I had another failure moment soon after that made me realize that I needed to do a reset. I was working at my past Google pace but without the same clear compass of what I was trying to deliver, who I wanted to do that for, and what I was going to learn from each opportunity.

Unfortunately, I had to learn the hard way, by watching one of my early clients self-destruct. I had been consulting for two early start-up cofounders who seemed to have all of the right pieces in place to be successful. These two guys had a lot of potential and a big idea that I thought was very promising, but right from the start I had a drastically different business plan in mind than they did.

They had very aggressive fundraising goals, and we had diverging opinions on how much money they should raise and from whom. I was also concerned that the business model was still unclear, the product concept was flimsy, and they were entering into a very competitive market.

I pushed them to focus on being first to market with a top-rate product and hiring the right talent, who were in high demand and came with a steep price tag. They felt strongly they would need to get investors quickly in order to hire for the technical talent they would need to be successful. So, one of the cofounders, who had taken on the role of CEO, focused on raising capital, while the other, who had become the CTO, focused on tech and patent development for the product.

The CEO was incredibly good at raising capital and got a thrill out of meeting with famous and influential people and increasing their early seed round as much as possible. They hired top talent and looked prime to compete in the now-saturated start-up market of AI. While the CTO was meant to be solely focused on the deep technical aspects of the product and filing patents, he was always jumping on a plane with the CEO, meeting wealthy potential investors.

The problem was that no one was actually running the company. No one wanted to do the "boring" foundational work of managing people, creating operational procedures, conducting day-to-day approvals, or developing growth strategy. The company did not have a leader. They had the titles of leaders, but the actual job descriptions of those roles didn't match with their passions or translate into how they wanted to spend their time.

They had raised a shocking amount of money without even a single product to offer or even a refined idea of what problem they wanted to solve in the world and who their customers would be. I expressed these concerns over and over only to be ignored, belittled, and then gaslighted. I have since watched the company crumble and lose many of their hard-earned assets and talented staff because egos prevented them from recognizing that they weren't playing to their strengths.

I see so many people chasing a status or title they think will meet with family and peer approval but that brings them no joy. They are distracted by a job description that sounds exciting, powerful, and outwardly impressive but that does not reflect what they want to do day in and day out. These victims of self-sabotage are often extremely smart, hardworking people who want the respect that they think the title brings but find the core responsibilities draining because they aren't aligned with what they are truly passionate about contributing.

Today, years after this early consulting experience, I can now see that while they suffered from unbridled ego, I was guilty of the other extreme, where I self-corralled my possible influence out of fear. Rather than being proactive about my doubts in the company's methods, I allowed their skepticism to silence me. I started to avoid their calls and stopped engaging with their projects rather than drawing a proactive line in the sand. In retrospect, it is obvious that this uncharacteristically withdrawn reaction to a challenge came from my fears of how to be impactful alone, without the Google reputation and machine behind me.

I gave in to the fear that I had no idea what I was doing, and I allowed others to shake my confidence in my instincts. I lost sight of my actual unique value-add and doubted my worth. I had to do something if I was going to survive being an entrepreneur.

CREATE A PERSONAL BUSINESS PLAN

This experience made me take a step back and take a hard look at myself and how I was managing my own career. I had taken on so many clients, and things escalated so quickly, that I couldn't implement procedures fast enough to keep up with all the accompanying demands. Somehow I had created a business where I had far too many people needing far too much of my time, and I could not keep up with it all to my usual standards.

I had a reality check with myself and realized that I needed to restart with a firmer foundation. The irony that I wasn't able to effectively manage my workload and create systems of management that would scale with the demands of my growth was not lost on me. I needed a heavy dose of my own business advice before I could be truly helpful to anyone else.

I finally sat down to have a thinking retreat and strategy session with myself, where I wrote a proper business plan and mission statement for what I wanted to accomplish in my work, and I realized that consulting was only one part of what I wanted to offer. This was an exercise I had done many times, even while working at Amazon and Google: I was building a road map for my personal progress. If I hadn't had the experience of doing that for myself while within the safety net of established companies, I'm not sure I would have been able to do that for myself while out on my own for the first time.

Know Your Mission

I realized that I needed to flesh out what I did and did not want in this next phase of my career before I could create my road map and be ready to help others do the same. I knew that I didn't want to feel like I had multiple bosses, projects that drained me, or a calendar that wasn't a true reflection of my priorities or values. I did want to focus on creating value, and that started with defining who I wanted to serve and what I was going to provide them.

I realized that I had created this situation for myself because I feared that I would have to take whatever luck brought me. I realized that rather than taking on any project that came my way, I could and must be selective and proactive with what I decided to put my name on and my time into. I started putting potential entrepreneur clients through a bit of a test before I would take the first meeting to be sure we were in full alignment on values, deliverables, and expectations. Then I would only agree to a three-month trial contract to see if we were a good fit before agreeing to an ongoing contract.

I wanted to work on projects where we had the same passion and impact goals. I started accepting only projects where the work and people aligned closely with my personal values. I wanted to work for companies that benefit their communities, provide growth opportunities for underrepresented entrepreneurs, or have the potential to revolutionize an industry. I chose to work only with entrepreneurs who are hungry to learn, humble enough to truly listen, willing to take calculated risks, and value their employees and mission above all else.

I created a mission statement that would become my true north and guide all of my business decisions going forward by answering the questions of who I was going to serve, why I wanted to do it, and how I would deliver it. I decided that my mission is to "create and empower underrepresented entrepreneurs globally to build the good we want to see in the world through actionable education and mentorship." With this in mind, choosing which clients and projects to take on as well as where to invest my time and resources is now easy and empowering. I want to be proactive in finding underrepresented voices to amplify, so that means I need to expand my circle of influence and get out of my comfort zone. I prioritize only projects that align with my values, even over monetary gain. And I spend my time and resources on creating active education with a global reach. This became my personal North Star, and the path has been easier and lighter ever since.

And then I cleared the slate and started again. The only client I kept on was the AgTech company, and I parted ways with everyone else while keeping the door open for ways to collaborate in the future. When my mission came into focus, so did my impact.

I realized that my former crutch of simply outworking everyone around me wasn't serving me anymore. I decided to out-*care* everyone instead. This was a subtle idea that led to a major mental pivot for me. If I out-care everyone, then I offer things to my work and clients that go beyond the projects, problems, or challenges I've been asked to solve. I prioritize the quality and insightfulness of my work rather than just the hours contributed to it or the end result. I look deeper into what they are really trying to solve, create, and contribute, and I am more creative on how I get immediately to the heart of that.

Claim a Seat at the Table

One of my most transformational projects as a solopreneur started before I had even left Google. I had spoken at the South by Southwest (or SXSW) conference in March of 2018 and noticed a very nice tweet about my talk afterward that shared some thoughtful takeaways. I responded and started an exchange with the author, Chris. He was based in England and had some very insightful perspectives on the material I had presented.

I would be working from the Google London office shortly after the conference, so Chris and I arranged to get together for a coffee to continue the conversation. I had no idea that that coffee meeting would eventually lead to him offering me my first seat on a board of directors six months later. Chris is a serial entrepreneur whose sincerity, vision, and natural mentor skills come through in every conversation. He is chairman of the board of directors for a customer relationship management (CRM) agency based in Bristol, UK, among many other roles.

Chris was scouting for a non-executive director for the company's board and wanted to bring in someone with a diverse perspective and more tech-focused background to help them with some of their long-term growth goals. He and his two partners—the CEO, James, and the CFO, Andy—had just done a management buyout of the company and wanted to really revolutionize it to be competitive in the new digital side of marketing. I think I literally laughed when he asked if I was interested in joining their board of directors. I knew absolutely nothing about CRM and felt like I didn't have the skills to contribute at that level yet.

It sounded crazy to bring in an American woman from Silicon Valley with no expertise in the marketing industry or solid connections in the community, but that was exactly the kind of outsider Chris envisioned being able to shake things up with a fresh perspective. It turns out that Chris knew the advantage of having a novice in the room and taught me that business lesson all over again.

I flew to Bristol to meet his business partners, feeling unsure how the meeting would go. However, by the end of dinner, something clicked between the four of us, and we just knew it was a risk worth taking. Serving on this board of directors was one of the most challenging and rewarding parts of my post-Google life transition. I had to translate my knowledge from Silicon Valley companies into applicable principles and lessons to fit a different industry, scale of growth, and European market. This has been a great gift that prepared me for several other rewarding client projects and board positions, but perhaps most important, I learned to trust my ability to contribute outside my tech bubble.

After my first year on this board, we did self-evaluations and team evaluations, which really helped me turn a corner in my confidence and improved the quality of my contributions. My feedback from the other board members was unanimous and clear: speak up! I had been so worried that I wasn't enough of an expert to contribute anything worth their time that I would occasionally wait unnecessarily to offer an opinion or suggestion unless I was called on directly.

On one critical board project, I was explicitly assigned the role of devil's advocate by James, the CEO, and was challenged to anticipate problems and poke holes in the proposed solution. This was an eye-opening exercise for me because I suddenly realized that I had a lot to say. I had just been waiting for permission to say it.

After working at Google for twelve years, I had become accustomed to having the depth of experience to offer expertise and firmly based recommendations. I had been waiting to have that feeling again before I really spoke up in board meetings. I had forgotten the lesson already learned from earlier in my career that my outsider, novice perspective was exactly what qualified me to speak up and ask the tough questions. That was *why* I had been given a seat at the table. Now I was in a role that valued my breadth of perspective and experience, rather than my depth of knowledge.

My exposure to the company amounted to a one-day visit each month, so it was challenging for me to glean the depth of knowledge I needed to give me the same confidence I'd had at Google. We pivoted our engagement and started meeting as a board by video for an hour every week, which gave me more context about the current company issues, what was going well, and what could use improvements, so that when we had our full monthly board meetings, I had foundational knowledge and was able to contribute more substantive advice.

With this encouraging push of honest feedback, I started asking more questions so I could understand the factors involved in each decision, and I started offering more suggestions based on what I had seen work well in similar situations at other companies. This took my contributions to a deeper level and helped build up my confidence that I could add real value to the leaders of any industry on any growth scale.

REMEMBER THAT STRENGTH FOLLOWS THE STRUGGLE

Once I clarified my business model and ideal client, I could then focus my energy into other parts of my life that I felt were holding me back. One of these major challenges was the fact that I was building a company in a new country. Spain easily delivered on my expectations of being an ideal place for reflecting and brainstorming. Every sight, sound, and taste I experienced in my new daily life gave me both joy and inspiration. However, I had underestimated the extreme culture whiplash I would experience when moving from Silicon Valley to a small coastal town in Spain.

The pace was slow everywhere—the banks, the restaurants, the flow of foot traffic. Did you know that the pace of foot traffic is directly correlated to the number of patents filed in that city? There is a measurable heartbeat to each city that correlates to the attitudes, urgency, and innovative tendencies of its inhabitants. I think that sums up perfectly why I experienced this change in pace so dramatically. A change in environment like this is charming when on vacation, but when you are on a mission to reinvent yourself, it can be a little jarring. And it turns out it was exactly the shake I needed to wake up my deepest desires.

I missed the pace of always being on an airplane and meeting powerful people on a regular basis. I needed to find a way to move past feeling lost and unproductive. I was suddenly a team of one without any resources beyond myself. The reality of being a solopreneur really sank in at this point. I needed to put myself back in the driver's seat and into the fast lane again.

Cultivating Humility

First, I needed to get my confidence and identity back. I found learning Spanish to be far more frustrating than I had expected. I learned several foreign languages when I was younger and spoke several fluently already, so I expected the learning curve to be familiar. It was not. Some of it might have been due to the age and elasticity of my brain: when I was twenty-one, I lived in Sweden and became fluent in Swedish in less than six months.

I had enough challenges going on in my life, and it was an infinite frustration for me not to be able to communicate clearly or create authentic relationships. I occasionally felt overwhelmed, lonely, and isolated because of my lack of fluency. I felt self-conscious about seeming boring because I was slow to talk at a party or uninteresting because it often felt not worth the effort to try and share a story when I couldn't deal with the humiliation of weaving together the four different past tenses in Spanish that would be necessary to communicate it.

After a while, I had to take a breath and remind myself not to be intimidated by the enormity of the task of learning this new language. I just had to start with small, manageable steps, and eventually all the pieces would come together. I started going to Spanish lessons for three hours every morning and was committed to being fully present in conversations with friends even when I understood very little of what they said. I spent a lot of time actively listening rather than tuning out and just looking at my phone when I wanted to do so the most.

I have had many humiliating moments while trying to learn Spanish. The best advice given to me about learning a language is that you must make one million mistakes in order to become fluent, so you might as well get them over with. You cannot skip that step. So, each time I make an embarrassing mistake or get lost in a fast-paced conversation, I remind myself that I've crossed off another mistake from my list on my way to fluency.

I have made mistakes that were so funny, the person I was speaking with laughed uncontrollably, right to my face. Like the time I tried to explain to my hairstylist why I arrived barefaced to my appointment when normally I wear makeup. I wanted to say that I hadn't had time to put on makeup (*maquillaje*) and instead I said I hadn't yet applied butter (*mantequilla*). Once she figured out what I was trying to say, she couldn't help but laugh at my mistake before regaining her composure. I won't pretend I didn't blush in embarrassment. It hurts to feel stupid. However, I absolutely bounce back when I think about how that moment got me one major step, or mistake, closer to my goal.

This is true of all the major goals I have set for myself. Failure is an essential part of the process. You can't skip that step—or those million steps—so you might as well get them over with. Nowhere has this been truer for me than in my career progression.

Set a Manageable Pace

At the start of 2020, I thought I finally had a strong plan for what I was going to be able to accomplish. I had really rewarding client relationships and finally felt the flow I had been missing from my Google years. I felt challenged but not overwhelmed. I even had a waiting list of companies that wanted to work with me, and I was spending a lot of my time thinking about how to better scale my consulting work to help more people without adding more hours to my workday. I had a full calendar of speaking events confirmed for the year and was also starting to organize a few events of my own, where I could focus on C-suite optimization and company-impact goal setting, and I'd started reaching out to potential attendees. And then the COVID-19 pandemic arrived.

On March 11, I flew from Spain to Austin, Texas, with plans to speak at the SXSW conference for the fourth time. At the last minute, the conference was canceled. To make matters worse, once I arrived in the States, the crisis in Spain suddenly became exponentially worse, and my return flights were canceled and the Spanish border was closed. I was stuck. I decided to fly to Seattle and wait it out with my family. I became really worried about the health and safety of my loved ones in both Seattle and Spain because they were in the original outbreak hot spots in the world. Thankfully, all of my loved ones remained healthy, and I started to shift my concern to my clients. I woke up nearly every day before five o'clock in the morning to connect with my European clients before shifting my attention to my US-based clients in the afternoon. All of this done from the bedroom I had had in high school.

Every single one of my clients found themselves in a huge pivot moment where we needed to adjust their business strategies, company policies, expenses, and workplaces just to survive. The entire world was in a moment of panic and overwhelm. I helped my clients set up systems for the CEOs to not only stay connected and present with their employees but also to be seen as confident leaders despite the feeling of making things up as they went.

What every single one of these leaders discovered was that what their teams needed most was for them to connect on a human level. The employees wanted to hear acknowledgment that things were hard and messy and frustrating. When leaders tried to be too perfect or confident, it had the opposite of the intended effect.

What brought the teams together was the shared hardship and human side of the situation. What became most important was increased transparency within the company and clear, consistent messaging. This was most true when navigating through difficult decisions of putting people on furlough or letting them go in order to keep the company afloat.

It is hard to keep a team motivated or plan a cohesive survival strategy when you aren't sure where the finish line will be or how to best plan a path forward. It reminded me of the spin class I regularly attend. Our usual instructor, Rebecca, consistently gives the class a clear overview of the challenges she's got in store for us across the course of the workout. At the beginning of a new music track, she might tell us that we're going to do three thirty-second standing sprints with sixty seconds of rest between each of them. That helps me pace myself and push myself harder during the sprints because I know I will be able to recover in between.

There was a week when Rebecca was on vacation and I did a workout with a substitute instructor. The workout was very similar to one Rebecca might lead, but this instructor didn't have the same habit of telling us in advance what we could expect; we just sprinted or climbed without knowing how long we would need to push ourselves before we would have relief. I noticed that my heart-rate monitor showed that my calorie burn after this substitute's class was significantly lower even than my average burn with Rebecca, although the workout structure was almost identical. The difference was that I hadn't known how to plan, so I was subconsciously conserving energy and not pushing as hard as I was otherwise capable of doing.

Like the pandemic challenge, the daily challenge of founding a company can be strangely similar to these workouts. Because no one knows when or if things will feel normal again, many usually high-performing people find themselves in a state of passivity or productivity paralysis as part of self-preservation.

Because of this experience, I have shifted my methodology with my clients, and I now create expectations of short, measured, controlled sprints whenever we are making major changes. I spend time laying the foundation and helping them understand what exactly is expected of them and for how long. This gives everyone a measurable amount of time to the finish line and clearly defined deliverables.

This mental shift has consistently made a huge difference in overall productivity and willingness to take risks and try some hard things. We don't always feel like we can accurately predict how we're going to approach a big growth goal, but we can be clear on what we are doing this week and this month to be successful in this new environment.

What is on everyone's mind globally is how to future-proof their careers and companies. There is a false sense of security in passivity.

It has been so liberating for me to spend the last several years working from anywhere. I do not miss my former three hours of daily commute or absurdly expensive rent in California. I now live two blocks from the Mediterranean and work from anywhere, anytime I want. I choose my clients, projects, and work hours myself, and I am enjoying my life more than ever because I am focused on doing only those things that I personally value and that bring me satisfaction. I have given myself permission to let go of anything that doesn't challenge me or align with my "why." This has given my life balance, fulfillment, and growth I could not have had any other way.

I have had to face the fact that in my lifelong pursuit of advancement, learning, and progress, I have created some unhealthy patterns that I need to now keep in check. Because I was always eager to earn a seat at bigger and bigger tables, I often volunteered for everything just to get noticed and have growth experiences. While this largely served me very well in the early parts of my career, I now know I need to acknowledge the negative side to always being the go-to person.

When I sought out being indispensable, I sometimes set myself up for burnout and frustration when I couldn't produce the quality of results I wanted because I had far too many commitments. Adam Grant, an organizational psychologist and professor at the Wharton School, has explained that, "If you love your job, people are more willing to ask you to do extra work unpaid—even if it is demeaning and not part of your role—and to sacrifice sleep and family time." Professor Grant calls this the passion tax. I have been the willing victim of this passion tax for an embarrassing percentage of my career, but now I am willing to start saying no.

Now that I'm further along in my career, I need to be careful of overcommitment syndrome and unintentionally crippling myself. I have tried to keep a long-term view of my career and recognized that I need to be strategic when I agree to do a sprint-effort project and for how long. There are times when that has been essential for advancement, but it's only worth it when you return to your steady marathon pace as soon as possible. If you try and push yourself constantly, you will burn out. Instead, find something that you desire so much that *it* pulls *you*. The momentum will remain, but the energy cost is much lower.

You are your most valuable asset.

CHAPTER 9 ROI SPRINT

Are there opportunities for you to repackage your skills today that will stretch you beyond your current circle of influence? Is your gut telling you that you were made for more? What is your personal mission for your life and work? What is your true north for what you want to learn and contribute, where you want to spend your time, and who you want to spend your life journey with? Can you set some new rules for engagement that will open you up to take some risks and find a more rewarding pace? What can you say "no" to today to make space for what brings you true fulfillment and a more sustainable pace?

Recognize: What are some ways that you can take your current skills, level them up, and repackage them to move you closer to your ultimate goals? Have you set yourself up as a victim of the passion tax?

Own: What steps could you take today to make your goals a reality? What distractions do you need to remove to get started? What buy-ins do you need to seek? What tasks are no longer elevating you but weighing you down?

Implement: Take that big first step today to get the momentum going!

CONCLUSION

I want to leave you with a well-kept secret about leveling up and claiming a more adventurous life. The bigger the bet, the easier it is. Really! I once went skydiving with my brother, Reed, and sister, Erin, to celebrate their birthdays which are a week apart in June. I had been bungee jumping before and absolutely hated every single second of that experience. I was so terrified that the guide had to literally push me off the platform (at my fearful request) because I couldn't make myself step off. It took a lot of convincing to get me to join my siblings for something I expected to be ten times worse.

The day of our jump, I kept waiting for the feeling of terror to arrive. Even when we put on our jump suits, watched the safety video, and signed the form acknowledging that what we were about to do could result in our death, I still felt calm. As we sat in the airplane at altitude and they opened up the door and my tandem guides inched us toward the edge, and my legs dangled outside the plane, I was simply excited.

We jumped out of the door, soon to be followed by my siblings, and I didn't feel like I was falling. I felt like I was flying. The earth didn't seem to be getting any closer as we plummeted, so my brain couldn't comprehend that I was falling—and fast! It wasn't until the first parachute opened, after what felt like an eternity of free fall, and I felt that first tug of a gravity-like force, that I had a tiny moment of fear before a return of exhilaration.

I think my career and all of life's big bets are a lot like skydiving. When the stakes are so high, the pace so fast, and the margin for error so small that I couldn't really comprehend it, I experienced a thrill rather than terror. I didn't know enough in those early stages to be appropriately afraid. And so I was brave. When I have experiences or take risks that feel more like bungee jumping than skydiving, the feelings of terror momentarily return. That is when I need to ironically make even bigger bets and aim even higher to get that feeling of flying again. I want to stay so high up that I'm not afraid.

I don't have any tattoos, but if I ever get one, I might consider one that reads *Gradatim Ferociter*, which is Latin for "step-by-step, ferociously." This phrase happens to be the motto of Jeff Bezos's space company, Blue Origin, but that's not the reason it connects with me. I think it is the perfect summary of the way I have chosen to live my life and shape my career—measured but fearless.

If there is any common thread in this unexpected life that I've had, it would be that each seemingly small moment or decision has had a ripple effect more profound than I ever could have imagined. If I had remained shy, stayed in my lane, and lived my life according to the advice of others rather than choosing to follow my own compass, I would have missed out on my life's greatest adventures.

I am not a person who is unapologetically bold and dismissive of conventions or outside opinions. However, I have learned to keep those influences in check and listen to my inner voice when it tells me that something special could happen if I take chances on myself. That's the secret. That's been the difference between an unfulfilling and an adventurous life.

I firmly believe that every single person is the best in the world at something. This is based on each of our one-of-a-kind DNA as well as our unique personal experiences. No one in the world is just like you, and so there is a unique opportunity for you to contribute something to the world that absolutely no one else can. The hardest part is daring to show up and be seen.

The harsh reality is that success is often not merit based. Some people just win because they are in the right place at the right time. Some are just plain lucky. However, the most successful and powerful people in the world all have a common denominator, which is that they were willing to put in the work and were bold enough to give themselves permission to make seemingly impossible dreams come true. That's the good and the bad of it. So if you're shying away from making a bold move because you think that others out there are smarter and better positioned to be successful than you are, I am here to tell you that that is not the case. Do not let that hold you back!

What if you decided today that taking risks is your new status quo? The best thing you can do is learn to find joy in the process of doing hard things and learning to be comfortable with being uncomfortable. Those are much bigger predictors of long-term success than pure talent.

In this new phase of my life and career, I am aiming for what I call the Moonshot Mindset. It takes a lot of investment, experimentation, and self-confidence to reach this stage, which terrifies, challenges, and thrills me. People often ask me what makes

Silicon Valley entrepreneurs different. I say it all comes down to the way they think.

All of the world-changing CEO managers I have worked with believe that they do not have fixed abilities, talents, or potential. They are confident that just because they haven't tried something before, that doesn't mean they won't be able to figure it out and be successful at it in the future. They actively invest in reinventing themselves almost daily.

There is a kind of superpower in those who are able to un-apologetically dream. Children come by this ability naturally. They live fully in the magic of limitless imagination and joy. Kids aren't embarrassed or apologetic for proclaiming that they want to be an astronaut and a veterinarian and a cowboy. This is because, unlike adults, they aren't self-defined by what they don't know or haven't yet experienced. Their learning compounds so quickly that any trajectory seems plausible. They are like a new-born person nearly every single day who is unshackled by what they were able to do yesterday.

I am fascinated and drawn in by those few adults in the world who are able to maintain this ability and live fully in that space of limitless future possibilities. It has been my life's privilege to surround myself with these dreamers and build my career while inspired by them. These people are rare, but I honestly do not believe that this needs to be the case. There are small things we can do to reawaken this innate ability within each of us, regard-less of our current tolerance for risk.

How much of your life is lived within your comfort zone? Really, let's do the math: What percentage of your day feels safe and comfortable, where you know how to do every task, can anticipate each problem before it arises, and are the expert in the room? And what percentage of your average day challenges you with projects and tasks you've never done before, where you are learning massive amounts of new things and are the least-authoritative voice in the room?

Most of us prefer to live our lives filled with tasks and experiences we are familiar with and that align with our strengths. The irony is that this seemingly safe zone is in reality a dangerous place to live for anyone who wants a life and career of adventure, impact, and growth. It is like a self-imposed jail. Our desire to feel consistently successful and safe keeps us within the confines of what we know we can do well and robs us of the freedoms and thrills of reinventing ourselves through challenges and struggles, which allow us to build the required strength to reach our potential. Spectacularly successful people spend most of their time pushing the boundaries of their expertise and are willing to learn through failure.

Through my professional experiences, I have learned that, no matter the life or career stage I am in, there are things I can do to put myself in the driver's seat. There is no feeling more debilitating than helplessness, the sense that you are unable to change your circumstances. I have been in the depths of that despair on numerous occasions, and the thing that pulled me out of it was my realization that I—and I alone—controlled myself and my reactions. I couldn't and can't control how others behave. I can't control the turns of the economy, global pandemics, illnesses, or whether other people will let me down. But I can always control my reactions to those things. It is liberating, even in times of extreme ambiguity, to realize that you and you alone are in charge of your trajectory in life.

When nearly everything in my life that had defined me was uprooted and replaced over the last five years, I clung to these rocks of truth:

Give yourself time. There are no set ages or timelines for life's stages or accomplishments. You can go back to school, change careers, up-level your ambitions, have kids (or decide not to), move to a foreign country, or pick up a new hobby. There is no wrong time to follow your inner compass.

Live your own life. The most miserable people I know made all the "right" choices to make their parents, friends, or society proud despite those things being in conflict with what they really wanted to do, be, or experience. You are accountable only to yourself. Make this decision sooner than later.

Do more of what you love. We only have this one life, so be sure to fill it with things that bring you joy and are personally meaningful. This can be defined by you and you alone. Have a clear understanding of your individual values, and center yourself around them every day.

Let go of other people's judgment. I've been judged by many people who erroneously assume I chose a career over having kids or that my marriage failed because of my ambitions. They do not know my heartaches. I have decided not to apologize for the life I have now or for the decisions I have made. I don't want to try and own other people's feelings. (This is a tough one for me!)

You can redefine failure. By some measures, I have had failed projects, failed speeches, a failed marriage, failed pregnancies, or a failed academic career. However, I see myself now as someone who is better having experienced those things because of the strength and empathy I built as a result. I wouldn't change my path even if I could go back and do things over again.

Be open to the unexpected. Life asked me to leave behind my dream job, my home, my country, my language, and nearly every earthly possession in order to find real happiness. I had to immerse myself in a new perspective in order to discover my path forward. You can choose to be brave enough to follow your unique path by taking measured chances and trusting yourself to figure things out when life gets hard.

Be present. I would have missed out on the greatest life lessons if I hadn't consistently paid close attention to the people, experiences, and challenges around me on seemingly average days. Inspiration and wisdom usually come in whispers, so you need to be willing to get lost in the present moment rather than being consistently distracted by the future or the exotically distant. There is a direct correlation between observing and learning.

Seek out high-quality people. Find people who challenge, lift, inspire, and value you. Do not settle. They are the greatest predictors of who you will become.

My hope is that you will join me in taking this journey of life step-by-step, ferociously. Make big bets on yourself! The world needs *you*!

ACKNOWLEDGMENTS

I will be forever grateful for the many influential lives that have become intertwined with mine and shaped me into a far better version of myself.

First and foremost, I would like to thank my bosses Jeff Bezos, Marissa Mayer, and Eric Schmidt for taking a chance on me and giving me an opportunity to be part of your journey and have experiences beyond my wildest dreams at both Amazon and Google. This book doesn't even begin to scratch the surface of what you have taught me, the adventures we have had together, and how much you mean to me personally.

Eric Schmidt, I cannot think of anyone who knows me professionally better than you! Thank you for your trust, leadership example, and vision, and for teaching me to "if at all possible, say yes!" I never imagined the many parts of this globe that our work would take us to! Thank you for including me in rooms with the most brilliant minds in the world and demanding I take a seat at the table. Our careers overlapping quite literally changed my trajectory in life. Thank you for your example of fearlessness, curiosity, and vision.

Marissa Mayer, I will always be grateful that you chose me to be a core member of your team. Thank you for teaching me to invest in the people around me, to take on challenges before I felt ready to perform them perfectly, and to build world-class teams. You have always been so generous with your friendship, mentorship, and influence. Your career and leadership continue to inspire me, and I only wish we could see each other more often! Thank you for your continued support and friendship!

Jeff Bezos, working for you changed the course of my life. You not only inspired me but showed me how to design my own fate and to (literally!) shoot for the stars. Thank you for giving me a chance to shine when I didn't feel worthy of it. Your booming laugh will always remain one of my favorite sounds. Thank you for the quarterly lunches off campus with our team. Some of my most cherished memories from Amazon and greatest business lessons came from that dedicated quality time together. You taught me to be *relentless* in the pursuit of my goals, despite my timid nature. Only you could have done that!

John Connors, thank you for being more than just my manager at Amazon. You were my mentor, guide, and dear friend. I would have failed without your investment and faith in me in those earliest years of my career. You taught me to be unflappable, confident, and humble, and to anticipate every need and to lead teams with love. I have used your methods and best practices every day of my career since.

Pam Shore, thank you for being an amazing manager, cheerleader, defender, and all-around incredible mama duck at Google!

Thank you for recruiting me to your team. Our time together as teammates was far too short, but I'm glad our friendship has been even longer!

To my Google family, I cherish all the crazy times we have had together and cannot imagine people I would have rather shared that journey with! I am especially grateful for the long-term friendships that developed, especially among the product team admins who remain an inspiring, grounding, hilarious, and just plain awesome part of my life. You are the true originals who saved my sanity, taught me to lead without formal power, and inspired me to reach higher. What a wild ride!

To my dearest team PED, you are now my phantom limb. Kim Cooper, I will be forever grateful that you joined my team and singlehandedly helped keep me from drowning in that first post-CEO year. Brian Thompson, thank you for taking a chance and moving from London to California based only on our video conference interview. I am so glad we were right about each other! Kim and Brian, you have taught me more than any other professional relationship. Thank you for your patience while I was learning to be a leader, for forgiving my missteps in the process, for the many talents you generously shared, for your sense of humor among the madness, and for your calm in the storm when my life came crashing down. You are my foxhole friends for life! And Jennifer Barth Vaden, thank you for being the fierce New York–based PED rock and for your grace under pressure and incredible resilience! I am sorry your part of the PED journey got cut in editing. We absolutely could not have survived this early journey without you, and you are a forever member of this team!

To my HarperCollins publishing team, I am so grateful that you were willing to break the mold of how the publishing process is "supposed to be done" at every single stage of the game with me. Thank you for taking a chance on me. I will never forget our first meeting with Jeff James, Sara Kendrick, and Matt Baugher, as we filled the conference room whiteboards with what became three book ideas—not just one! Sara, thank you for your insights, guidance, and editing, and for enduring three entirely different versions of this book. You have understood my journey and message from the beginning, before I could even do it for myself. Sicily Axton, thank you for being willing to take an unconventional approach to marketing and promoting this book. I couldn't have asked for a better publishing team!

To my incredible book agent, Steve Troha at Folio Literary Management, thank you for seeing potential in my crazy life story. I never imagined that years later, you would still remember it and say my name out loud to HarperCollins and start this amazing opportunity for me. The value of your mentorship, friendship, and guidance over the past few years cannot be overstated. Plus, you're just truly amazing, and I am honored to consider you a friend now too.

RoseMarie Terenzio, I will owe you forever for not only introducing me to Steve but for your mentorship as a fellow author. This book literally would not exist without you! I am glad that I was able to transform from the "Google machine" to your close friend! Thank you for the many evenings we spent together while I was reinventing myself in New York City that sweltering summer—and the many years beyond.

Vickie Sokol Evans, you are hands down the architect of this stage of my career. Thank you for seeing, cultivating, and mentoring the talents you saw in me long before I fully believed in them myself. I am so lucky to have traveled across five continents with you, laughing, learning, and reinventing myself by your side. Not even cancer could stop you from creating opportunities for me to be on bigger stages. I do not know anyone more generous and thoughtful than you! You push me to be my best self every day!

Lucy Brazier, thank you for introducing me to your global audiences, for mentoring me as a startup founder, for your generous friendship, and for starting me off in my new life in Spain! You are an inspiration to and loved by people all across the world because of your selfless leadership and kind spirit. Bless you!

To my husband, Toni, thank you for always being proud of me, cheering on my insatiable drive to do and be more, and for never once complaining about how much this book writing process took over our lives. You are an amazing man, my dearest friend, and an inspiring entrepreneur. I have never met anyone who has your eye, talent, and instinct for seeing and creating beauty in the world the way that you do. Te quiero!

To my parents, Kim and Tammy, thank you for teaching me the values of hard work, selfless service, and dreaming big through your examples. Thank you for encouraging and supporting my education and for creating a family environment of joy, love, and service. To my six siblings, LaDawn, Candice, Erin, Reed, Blake, and Mickayla, I am so grateful that I have never needed to look beyond my own home for friendship, laughter, and love. Whether it's been Sunday popcorn and ice cream, producing plays in our garage, road trips counting cows, exchanging letters while living abroad, graduations and birthdays, jumping out of airplanes, welcoming in new in-laws and babies, you are always at the center of my most cherished memories. I am so proud of each of you and the amazing people you are. You inspire me!

Keith, I would not have done any of this without having you as my partner for so many years. Thank you for being my biggest supporter while I was figuring out the woman I wanted to become. You were the only witness to so many critical moments of my life, both professionally and personally, and gave me the courage to continue. I am glad that you signed and lived up to the friendship contract your dad wrote for us so many years ago. Ti voglio bene!

Andrew Postman, thank you for being my writing partner for the original spec of this book and helping me craft the framework for telling my story. Your concept of the ROI became a pillar idea within the final version. Thank you for remaining a resource and colleague when I went crazy and decided to write this on my own. Your edits and thoughtful questions were essential in the process of creating this book.

Steven Levy, I am honored by all the support you have offered me along my career evolution. I never imagined that when we met, while you were embedded with the Google APM trip around the world, that one day you would write an endorsement for my book and be a guest on my podcast. Your support and willingness to take a chance on me inspires me to pay it forward to other entrepreneurs.

Scott Duke Kominers, you have been an invaluable resource and instant friend. Thank you for your edits, support, and observations while I was finalizing this book. Your endorsement and support is a true honor. I have learned so much from you and look forward to more collaborations to come!

Pablo Rodriguez, you are one of the very few people who understand the challenges I've experienced over the last few years of working in Silicon Valley but living in Spain. Thank you for being my inspiration that it can be done and how I can have the best of both worlds. Your endorsement here means so much to me. I hope to be able to work together on many more global projects.

To all my post-Google consulting clients, I want to thank you for learning and growing with me while I was figuring out how to communicate and translate my Silicon Valley lessons to global entrepreneurs of all industries and scales of growth. I have learned more from you than you can possibly imagine.

To my dear friends at Armadillo, Chris, James, and Andy, I feel a huge sense of gratitude for your trust in me. I am so glad you thought outside the box and invited me to join your board of directors. I have learned so much from our work together and friendships. I look forward to many more milestones and collaborations to come!

I feel so grateful for all the many amazing educators across my life who took the time to help me discover, cultivate, and improve my talents. Ms. Jenkins, thank you for the eighth grade creative writing class that first inspired me to want to become a writer. Ron Mahan, thank you for being a positive force in my life during junior high and inspiring me to believe that I could be someone special and of significance. Professor Christine Ingebritsen and Professor Ann-Charlotte (Lotta) Gavel Adams at the University of Washington, thank you for investing in me and helping me turn my passion for global politics and Scandinavia into a career that exceeded my wildest expectations.

I want to give a deep thank you to several special friends, who were there in critical moments when I needed a friend the very most: Diana Ly, Reggie Love, Esther Sun, Monica Gnanadev, Alexis Weller, Rhett Weller, Teddi Thosath, Nicole Sandler, and Silvia Schiavinato. I will always be grateful to you!

I could not have navigated the earliest stages of setting up my company in Spain without the extremely talented partners at Workhouse Collective, Lucy and Guy! Thank you for seeing my vision, crafting my brand image, advising on critical early messaging, and being all-around amazingly talented people who never fail to make me feel like a rock star.

Jessica Bataille, thank you for sharing your beautiful office with me while I wrote and rewrote my book! I don't think I could have done it without that dedicated writing space and incredible Mediterranean sea view! Thank you for your continued generosity and friendship, which inspires me to focus on creating beauty in my life and work!

And finally, an enormous thank you to my literal employee number 1, Rebecca Hopwood! Becky, thank you for taking the chance and joining my startup as my very first employee. This book, my company, and my productivity in Spain never would have happened without you. Thank you for jumping with both feet into this chaotic startup life and for not only creating order and structure but also beauty and joy. Not only are you incredibly capable, but I cannot imagine having more fun with anyone! You are one of the most talented people I've ever worked with, and after reading this book (a few million times now), I know you know what a high bar that is. You are truly exceptional, and I am so honored to be on this journey together!

INDEX

ABOUT THE AUTHOR

Ann Hiatt spent the first fifteen years of her career working at Amazon and Google, starting in the early 2000s. She is now a leadership consultant with CEO clients all over the world. Ann is a native of Seattle but considers herself a global citizen. She has lived and worked in Tampa, Anchorage, Seattle, Stockholm, San Francisco, London, New York, and Valencia. She was a student of international studies and Scandinavian studies at the University of Washington and began a PhD program in Scandinavian studies at UC Berkeley before returning to tech. After two decades in Silicon Valley, Ann now lives on the Mediterranean coast of Spain near Valencia. *Bet on Yourself* is her first book.